Looking Back

Anthology of Short Stories

Looking Back – Anthology of Short Stories
A project developed by Nazar Look
Attitude and Culture Journal of Crimean Tatars in Romania
www.nazar-look.com

Looking Back

Anthology of Short Stories

Compiled by Taner Murat

Editura StudIS, Iaşi, 2013

Editura StudIS
adicenter@yahoo.com
Iasi, Sos. Stefan cel Mare, nr.5
Tel./fax: 0232 – 217.754

Descrierea CIP a Bibliotecii Naţionale a României
MURAT, TANER
Looking Back, Anthology of Short Stories /
Antologie de naraţiuni contemporane / Taner Murat.
Vatra Dornei : StudIS, 2013

ISBN 9786066244480

ISBN-13: 9786066244480
ISBN-10: 6066244485
BISAC: Literary Collections / General
Illustration and cover design: Elif Abdul
On the cover: "Sorrow", © Sagida Siraziy (Sirazieva),
https://www.facebook.com/profile.php?id=100004327597168

Consilier editorial: Dranca Adrian
Secretar editorial: Moroşanu Paul

Pre-press, tipar digital şi finisare:
S.C. ADI CENTER SRL
Şos. Ştefan ce Mare, nr. 5
Tel.: 217 754

Tantra Bensko **CARLY BERG** *Ute Carson* TONY CONCANNON Rudy Ch. **Garcia**

Margaret Karmazin JAMES D. REED W. *Jack Savage* TOM ·ria

Manish Singh Hollis Whitlock Samuel K. Wilkes Abigail Wyatt ON

Tony Concannon RUDY CH. GARCIA Margaret Karmazin **JAMES** \GE

Tom Sheehan BHADAURIA MANISH SINGH Hollis Whitlock igail

Wyatt Tantra Bensko Ute Carson **TONY CONCANNON** *Rudy C* ET

KARMAZIN JAMES D. REED **W. Jack Savage** TOM SHEEHAN Bhada LIS

WHITLOCK Samuel K. Wilkes Abigail Wyatt Tantra Bensko C non

RUDY CH. GARCIA *Margaret Karmazin* JAMES D. RE ·m

Sheehan BHADAURIA MANISH SINGH Hollis Whitlock SAMUEL K. W att

Tantra Bensko Carly Berg Ute Carson Rudy Ch. Garcia M IN

JAMES D. REED W. JACK SAVAGE Tom Sheehan B gh

HOLLIS WHITLOCK Samuel K. Wilkes ABIGAIL WYATT Tantr Ute

Carson Tony Concannon Margaret Karmazin **JAMES D. REED** OM

SHEEHAN Bhadauria Manish Singh **Hollis Whitlock** SAMUEL K. WILK A

BENSKO Carly Berg Ute Carson Tony Concannon Rudy Ch. (·

JACK SAVAGE Tom Sheehan BHADAURIA MANISH SINGH ·

Wilkes ABIGAIL WYATT Tantra Bensko CARLY BERG Ute Carso udy

Ch. Garcia Margaret Karmazin W. Jack Savage **TOM SHEEHA** ish

Singh HOLLIS WHITLOCK Samuel K. Wilkes **Abigail Wyatt** TANTR TE

CARSON Tony Concannon Rudy Ch. Garcia Margaret Ka Tom

Sheehan **BHADAURIA MANISH SINGH** Hollis Whitlock igail

Wyatt **Tantra Bensko** CARLY BERG Ute Carson TONY CONCA cia

Margaret Karmazin JAMES D. REED W. Jack Savage Bhada IS

WHITLOCK Samuel K. Wilkes ABIGAIL WYATT Tanti UTE

CARSON Tony Concannon RUDY CH. GARCIA Margaret Karmaz W.

Jack Savage Tom Sheehan Hollis Whitlock **SAMUEL K. WI** yatt

TANTRA BENSKO Carly Berg **Ute Carson** TONY CONCANNON Rud RET

KARMAZIN JAMES D. REED W. Jack Savage Tom Sheeh ngh

Samuel K. Wilkes **ABIGAIL WYATT** Tantra Bensko CARLY ny

Concannon RUDY CH. GARCIA Margaret Karmazin JAMES D. RE age

Tom Sheehan Bhadauria Manish Singh Hollis Whitlock Abigail KO

Carly Berg UTE CARSON Tony Concannon **Rudy Ch. Garcia** MES

D. REED W. JACK SAVAGE Tom Sheehan Bhadauria Manish Singh Hollis Whitlock Samuel

Photo: Tommy Bensko

Tantra Bensko

california, usa
http://lucidmembrane.weebly.com/

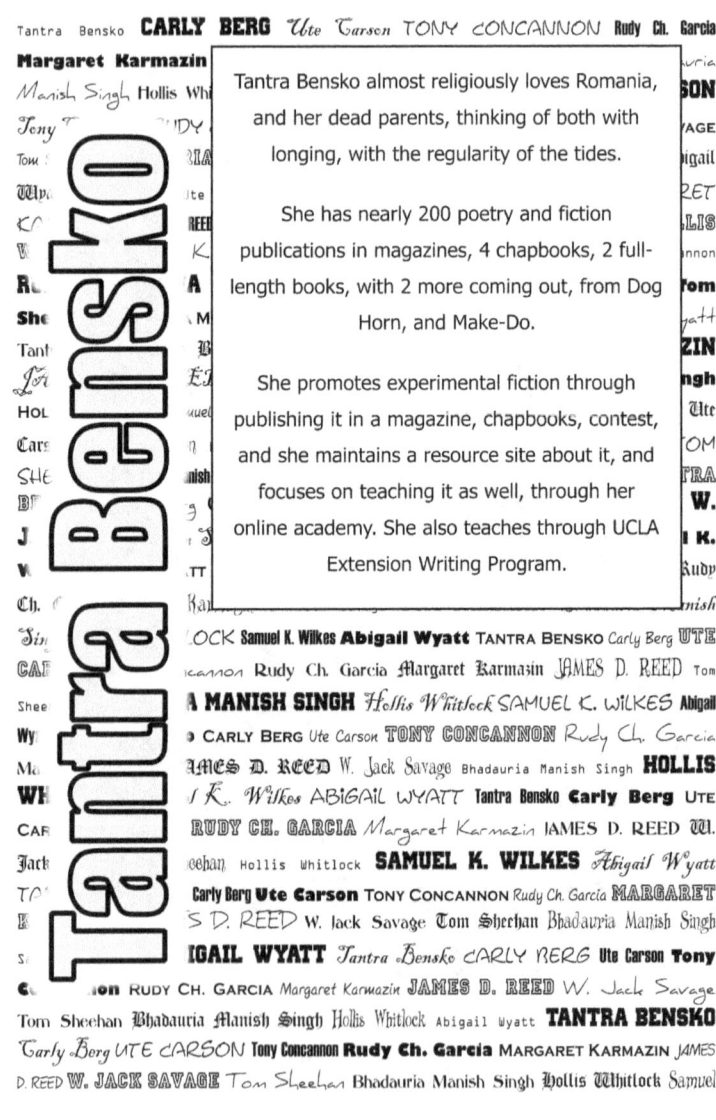

Tantra Bensko almost religiously loves Romania, and her dead parents, thinking of both with longing, with the regularity of the tides.

She has nearly 200 poetry and fiction publications in magazines, 4 chapbooks, 2 full-length books, with 2 more coming out, from Dog Horn, and Make-Do.

She promotes experimental fiction through publishing it in a magazine, chapbooks, contest, and she maintains a resource site about it, and focuses on teaching it as well, through her online academy. She also teaches through UCLA Extension Writing Program.

8

White Arms

The albino murders were never solved, because anyone who told on the killers would be made into soup. Any albinos in the tribe were considered to have magical arms and legs, useful for making everything happen that would not happen if they lived.

So people chopped them off.

Their families hid the the albinos the best they could. But there was almost nothing to hide them with in the landscape of sun and dirt. The albinos peeled from the sun on listless skin. Their lips cracked and trees were their saviors.

White Arms

When the tribesmen finally found them, and stole their limbs, very little changed. But any good luck that happened to them, they claimed must have come from the white arms and legs they swung around to the sky.

The albinos' mothers buried them in one special grave, and talked among themselves in ways no one else could. They said their dead children were all one child. They were all one creature of delight, coming to them for short times, here and there, sometimes many at once, sometimes twins. They said they were like different trees with one root system. Or like mushrooms.

They were like a ghost of the moon, a willow of the wisp, a sorrow not soon forgotten, a rain cloud with the face of forever. They blessed their mothers with secrets. The secrets they never told anyone else, not even their men.

The albino arms and legs once used up and starting to decay were stuck on sticks far away from the tribe. Black birds sat on top of them, devoured their magic.

The birds ate none of the animals the tribe raised for food for weeks each time after they ate their fill of secrets. It was believed to be good luck coming from the magical sacrifice.

The mothers dreamed of a giant childlike cloud that rained them a better season than before. They also dreamed of albino wars, of all the men who chopped the arms and waved them laid to dust.

Identical twin albinos who did everything together, said everything together, while leaving their dusty treehouse one day, were grabbed and dragged down and one of them butchered. The other one ran away.

Her dead sister's whiteness compounded inside her, and she became they. Not only they with her sister but they with all the other albino torsos.

Her arms and her legs gathered the magic of all those who had flailed. Her whiter trunk glared with the

11

anger of a dozens of ghosts merged into one. She roared with air and flew with on toes. She surprised 3 men at their bath in a pit they had dug in the outskirts. She recognized them well. She yelled.

And she flung the dirt in so fast, as the storm broke and turned it to mud, and the black birds pecked their eyes. She beat the killers with branches as they tried to escape, and the tradition of the albino murders ended. She was white with yellowing hair and sea-foam eyes. She who lived to be the first albino elder. She never told anyone it was she who mudded the men to death.

The only ones who chased her to the pit to watch what happened were the mothers. And they quietly grew an outskirts garden moist with dew, and tall white asparagus.

* * *

Papa's Song

It isn't so much that the ball of laughter killed my father, as that it was so pretty, and fuchsia. It isn't so much that it made me want to touch it, and fondle it, when I was home alone. Me, with the delicious, white-hot liquid luxurious red grabby ball of laughter under the table, rolling with its furriness, holding onto it and kicking it with my legs, like a hot cat being tickled.

It'd attacked Papa regularly long before it killed him, and I ignored it, like I ignored his obsession with Tutti Frutti ice-cream I also ignored him going on about the "willowy" girlfriends with "windswept hair," who

Papa's Song

worked in chicken houses and junk yards, and asked, when he met them, if he would like to get married in a couple weeks. Asking -- what happened to his money if I died, and then -- what happened to his money if my son died. Well, it was when the last chicken-girlfriend told him a secret, whispered it into his ear, that he laughed so hard, his tears were so big they burst his tear ducts, his heart, his 500 pounds of flesh, his money.

The ball of laughter had overtaken him most often at the dinner table, and turned his face red, as it bounced up and down inside him. You'd swear on a thousand foreign things that it was the sound of him crying. He'd wipe tears. But he was laughing, red, higher than the sound of fairies on a summer's day. Tinkling, like   cowbells. HUHHHHHHHHHUHHHHHHHHHUHHHHHH!

He reminisced about playing the cowbell in school band, and only knowing when to hit it because the conductor pointed to him each time. Ding!

He sang like a tuneless mosquito as I cooked complex courses of this and that, this and that, which I got all wrong when he, bouncing up and down on his legs, snapped his fingers out of rhythm. I wanted to tell him he could cook for himself, if he was going to make my ears vibrate and make me burn desert. The giant pot of desert bubbling just for him. I laughed instead.

I only once dreamed of him, 10 years after he died. Imagine this 6 foot 5 foot perfectly round man on stage in an auditorium made of dark, his black hair combed back and greased, in a purple suit, sitting on a chair with a spotlight on the giant empty. The musicians, in the pit, playing deep and slow, welling, violas, bass, trombone, heads banging. They stop. And he, who has never sung a real song, a bearable set of notes in his life, sings a capella the strangest wordless tune imaginable beyond the limits of the world of the living, an echoing falsetto.

And falls over dead. Silent. And laughing inside my heart so hard he seems so very much like really he is crying.

* * *

15

Mama

I figure my mother is not really there, because she's dead. "No, I'm not," she says.

"Yes, you are."

"I'm not." Her head flies off in anger, zooming across the room, getting smaller optically as it goes. Then, it jolts back, flying onto her neck, but overshooting, not attached in alignment with it. Off-center. It hasn't regained its regular size.

"Yes, you are."

I leave her to believe what she wants, and I resurface the table some more, giving it an antique look by hitting it with chains, before I put on a new coat of color that makes it old.

"Do it to me," she says.

"What?"

"Do it."

So, I rough her up with sand paper, and hit her with chains, making dents. She examines her surfaces, tidily and efficiently, indicating the spots most in need of filling in with scratches and scrapes.

"You died too young. You were so beautiful."

"You're welcome," she says. She turns her head and blushes. I can tell she doesn't want to agree to her dead status, but can't turn down the gratitude.

"Do you want some cherry varnish?"

"That would be very pretty."

Mama

She looks so natural in deep red. It makes it hard for her to move, but she's pretty stiff anyway. "I miss you," she says.

I cry. She doesn't. She's blowing on her surfaces, and unfortunately, blows out her dentures, which stick in the varnish just as it's setting. Now, her teeth are stuck to her right shoulder. "You're still the best, Mama. The very best."

* * *

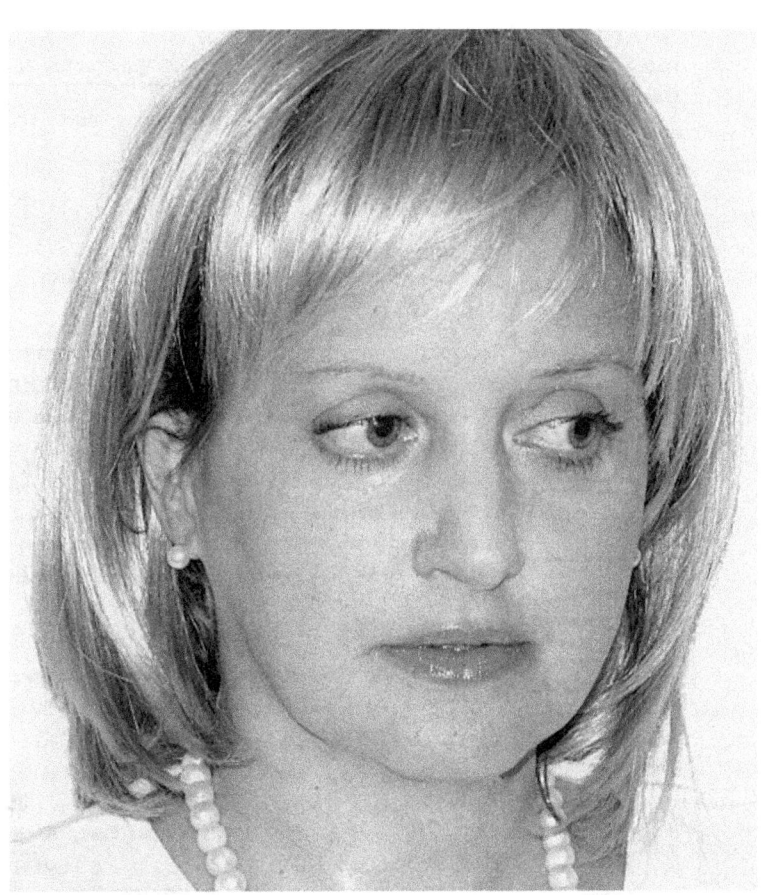

Carly Berg

texas, usa

Carly Berg is a dark cloud hovering above sunny Houston.

Her stories appear here and there.

She is at work on a book of interrelated flash stories.

20

Bringing Back Beulah

It was the summer of Ouija boards and spell-casting and levitations that almost worked. We half-dozen little girls passed the long, hot days in the cool basement bomb shelter, scaring ourselves silly.

One Saturday, my dad came down and found us doing our thing, it was the Ouija board that time. He got really mad. He said to never, ever play with the supernatural because that was playing with fire. It was inviting the devil into your life. He said we were only allowed to do Christian things, not devil things.

Bringing Back Beulah

My mom and dad got in a big fight about it. She said he was paranoid and repressed and we were just playing. Besides, The Church was part of The Establishment, who was invited to stick it. He said she needed to get off her neurotic campaigns and supervise the children appropriately while he worked all day.

Me and my sisters huddled together in the bomb shelter, sick over the fight, but honored to be taken so seriously. We believed our mom. Another girl had to bring her Ouija board over, because my dad threw ours in the trash. That was the summer Aunt Beulah died.

She was really Great Great Aunt Beulah, and she scared the sass out of us. Her voice was somewhere between Kentucky bourbon and peacock screech. She'd watch the fights on TV and pound her fists all the way down to the floor, screaming at the black and white screen, "Why, you son of a bitch! You dirty bastard!" The other ladies- my grandma, and aunts, and great aunts, and great great aunts- they were nice.

One of Aunt Beulah's eyes was a mashed potato. There was a big white lump, all taped over. We had to go to her house once. It was the oldest house in the world and it smelled like Vick's Vaporub. She drank skin milk, which was the grossest thing I had ever heard of.

There was a baby crib with some horrible dolls in it and she made me and my sisters play with them. They were so old, whoever had gotten them new was probably dead. The thought thrilled us deeply, but not in a way that made us want to hold them. More like the bubonic plague, to be studied and savored from afar.

Aunt Beulah never had children. When she was young, her husband had put his head in the oven and died. I pictured it like on the Shake 'n' Bake commercial, where the lady shakes the meat in the bag of breadcrumbs first. We thought Aunt Beulah played with the horrible dolls herself; why else would she have them?

She died. The nice ladies chittered that my mom shouldn't have brought us children to the wake, but my mom always did everything my grandma didn't like. My mom took us up to see The Body, as she was then called. I'd say Aunt Beulah was the one in a crib then. She had

Bringing Back Beulah

on a long, dark dress and a rosary was twisted around her hands. Her hands and face didn't look real, but she still had her mashed potato eye.

Getting to see a real dead person was groovy. My friends couldn't wait to hear about it. I had a cold, icky feeling in my stomach at bedtime afterwards, though. My mom let me stay up late looking at Highlights and National Geographics.

Our supernatural summer progressed to séances. Aunt Beulah was the only dead person we knew, so she was our only choice of who to bring back from the dead. If we had a different choice, we would have taken it.

My older sister took my dad's lighter and lit the smiley face candle she had been allowed to buy with her allowance, after she'd promised not to light it. My younger sister said she was going to tell. Everybody else said she couldn't play, then. And besides, we'd all say she was the one who lit it. So, she took it back.

We sat in a circle, me and my sisters and three other girls, ages five to ten. My older sister said the

24

ceremony things and then we all had to go around in a circle and say some other things, and then we chanted. Bring Beulah Back. Up With Beulah. My mom had taken us to hold signs and chant something with a whole bunch of people once, so we were going with that. We had decided not to wave signs around because this was more solemn, like at church.

The smiley turned to liquid yellow with black swirls in its jar and we kept on chanting until I was lost in the rhythm of it and under a spell myself, watching the flame and chanting with the others. Bring Beulah Back. Up With Beulah. Bring Beulah Back. Up With Beulah.

She came back.

She swirled up from the ground, like a genie out of a bottle, in the center of our circle. Her dress was the dark one from her funeral, and she was swinging the rosary down to the floor like the boxing was on. She was not solid though, more like waxed paper, but in her real colors. Suspended up in the air, she waved like a curtain in a breeze.

Bringing Back Beulah

The chanting stopped. The other girls fell all over each other, screaming. When I could catch my breath, I screamed too.

We bolted up the steps, stumbling over each other, and kept running until we were out in the bright, hot sunlight.

The candle was still burning. We sent my little sister in to tell on us for lighting it. My mom would go downstairs and blow it out.

My older sister and I got grounded for playing with fire. We also weren't allowed to play in the basement for the rest of the summer. Not that we wanted to; the basement was never the same secure space after that. In fact, every space was a bit less secure from then on, after coming to understand that people really do leave this world. And come back.

* * *

Fat Pat

Pat waited until the new home health aide left the room. As she opened the bag, her pleasure grew. Hot fried chicken perfumed the air. The blessed, golden taste!

She munched her way through the bucket of crunchy thighs, drumsticks, wings. Potatoes, whipped thick and covered in gravy. Flaky biscuits. Corn on the cob, wrapped in individual yellow sleeves that sealed in the melted butter. Each ear slid out of its package like a gift. She washed it all down with sweet, icy root beer.

Fat Pat

Afterwards, she lay back to drift on lovely dreams of picnics with friends, restaurants with dates, and being thin. The aide spoke on her cell phone from Pat's small living room.

"Girl, she's nasty. Reminds me of a damn hippo. Too fat to get out of bed! I have to change her Pampers. No, I ain't kidding."

Pat had been fat all her life. The other kids had called her hippo, pig, nasty, stinky. No one ever wanted to be her friend. She was nasty. Tears rolled down her big face.

"The doctor said she's gonna have a heart attack any minute. Yep, if she don't start that diet right now. Maybe even if she does."

Black terror seized Fat Pat, spun her mind crazy. Unless that was her heart acting up again. Or her high blood pressure, or diabetes. Diet. Die. The words sounded the same.

"Shoot, I wonder how they'll get her out of here. Bring a crane and bust out the damn wall, I guess."

After Pat's mother died, they pushed her onto the floor. They dragged her out on blankets. Her head had thumped down the apartment stairs. Mother and food were her friends, and Mother was dead.

"She throws a fit if I don't bring her a week's worth of food for a meal. Home Health says give her what she wants. No, I ain't kidding. Girl, I got her a family sized KFC a while ago, with all the sides, too. Hold on. If she's asleep, I'll take a picture."

Pat hid under the covers. Click. Click.

"Well, she had the sheet over her head. Look at the size of the lump in the bed, though, and the mess from her dinner. Nope, I didn't eat any, all hers. Oh good, it's six o'clock. I can't take no more today. Disgusting. Mmm-hmm."

The apartment door closed and, mercifully, it was quiet. The social worker had tried to get someone to come at night. The state said no, Pat was at the limit of her benefits. Any more cost, and she'd have to go to the nursing home.

Fat Pat

She checked that her medical alert device was on, and that her self-protection knife was in easy reach in the nightstand drawer. After hitting the tv remote, she opened a large bag of Ruffles. Crunchy delights! Pat grew lighter with each bite. Farther from the bedsores, better able to breathe. Loved. Pat's mouth was a delicate instrument. The crackle of chips, music to her tired soul.

The reality show, Fat, came on. "James Jefferson, from Texas. Eighteen years old and weighs 653 pounds," the thin blonde hostess said. Pat tapped the remote, wanting to watch and also wanting not to. The boy lived here in Houston, bless his heart.

Later, deep in the wild space between wake and sleep, Pat's doctor arrived. "It is time," he said. "Diet or die. Which do you choose?" He held her knife above her, poised to stab.

She floated out of herself, and knew it was real. Her new self, thin and blonde like the reality show hostess, snatched the knife away from her doctor, and he vanished.

texas, usa

The new self twirled in front of the dresser mirror, giddy. She touched the sharp angles of her cheeks, her slender wrists, her tiny waist. She still gripped the knife in her other hand.

Fat Pat said, "Don't... please." She wheezed between words.

The new thin blonde beheld the grotesque humanoid on the bed, the great Beluga of pain and shame. The air was heavy with sweat, faint bathroom mess, and acetone diabetes breath.

Pat's eyes shone in the darkness. The thin blonde felt deep pity for the poor creature. Yet, Fat Pat would soon be gone. Would the new self go, too? Choose.

The new self shut off her mind. With all her strength, she plunged the knife into Fat Pat.

Her hand slipped on the blade. Her blood mixed with Pat's and she screamed. It was done. The thin blonde slid to the floor. The medical alert people called. The machine picked up, someone had pushed the device's button. Sirens wailed outside. She scooted

Fat Pat

under the bed, all the way to the wall. They kicked in the door. Made noise. Swarmed the room. Took pictures. Click. Click.

She lay still under the bed and sucked her thumb. On the count of three, they rolled Fat Pat's carcass off the bed. She crashed, on blankets laid on the floor. The floor shook.

They dragged Pat away on the blanket sled. The thin blonde imagined that the head thumped down the building stairs.

All was mercifully quiet. She stole out of the dingy apartment, and twirled in the moonlight, free at last.

* * *

The Last Supper

Earl dozed, cozy by the fire, while his mother sat knitting nearby. The savory aroma of Sunday dinner filled the bungalow. His wife clattered about, mashing potatoes and stirring gravy.

"How long 'til we eat?" He could almost taste the hot roast beef.

It was not his wife who answered him, but Nancy, the hospice aide. "Not too much longer," she said. "Do you need another blanket?"

33

The Last Supper

He didn't reply. Nancy whispered to Earl's daughter, Terri, "Hospice patients often think they smell meat roasting. It's the darnedest thing."

"That is strange." Terri put down her Sunday newspaper and spread the extra blanket on top of her father's bedcovers. Nancy's perched on the sofa. Terri, in the rocking chair that had been her mother's, by the window.

The late afternoon sunlight colored the room pink, adding to the surreal feel for Terri. She'd last been home three years ago, for her mother's funeral. Now her father's deathbed replaced the living room coffee table. Outside, the husk of her childhood swing set rusted in the snow.

Earl plucked at the blankets. "I'm hot."

"Sorry, Father." Terri removed the extra cover.

"Get my cane and my hat and pull the goddamned car up the driveway! I'm going home. I'm going to St. Louis."

Patients always wanted to return to their childhood homes. Nancy pushed the button to increase his morphine drip.

"Here you are, Father. Here's your cane. And here's your hat." He didn't see well anymore, so Terri placed the items in his hands. She cringed when he took the cane.

Nancy's expression changed, but straightened immediately, as if she had corrected herself.

"Get the goddamn car."

"The car's coming," Nancy said. "Here, take a sip." She held the water glass, guiding the straw to his lips.

Earl batted the cup away.

He was cute, in a pitiful way, scowling, clutching his hat and cane. This patient exhibited agitation when his physical discomfort increased. Nancy pushed the morphine drip again.

The Last Supper

The roast scented the air. Earl resumed dozing by the fire. His mother knitted a scarf for him.

"Uh-oh. Someone turned off the lights."

Terri startled at his raised voice.

"We'll get them turned back on. Don't worry," Nancy said.

"He'll be passing soon," she whispered to Terri.

Passing the rolls soon, you mean. Earl laughed, but did not remember why. His mother said the circus would be coming to town. Would Earl like to go to Barnum and Bailey? "Peachy keen."

Someone tapped his shoulder. She had a girl. He handed out cigars with false enthusiasm. "Have a cigar." He had wanted a son.

Terri's throat closed. The newspaper print jumped around. He used to smack her with a rolled up paper, how you'd smack a dog. He slapped her and whipped her over anything, for not finishing her dinner, for not saying "please" or "thank you." She'd been a

36

timid, well-behaved little girl., Unsure of her evaluation of events, she re-played his punishments over and over . What hurt most was that she turned against herself. After all the times he beat her up, she sat there, smiling at him. Even in adulthood, she played along, a gutless worm. It would be too late to ever take her own side against him.

"Are you all right, Terri? No, hon. Those big breaths make it worse. Here, rock in your chair and breathe slow. In through your nose, and out through your mouth. Good."

The pink light faded to mauve. Earl slept. Nancy said, "I can't give you any meds, hon, but do you have over-the-counter sleeping pills? They would calm you."

"That's a good idea. Let me check."

Terri came back from the bathroom a few minutes later. "No sleeping pills in the medicine cabinet. But it's a good idea. Hey, you wouldn't... oh, nevermind."

The Last Supper

"Get you some, you mean? Sure. I'm staying tonight, so I need to run home and grab my things anyway. I've already called my boss."

"That would be great. Staying over and the pills. Thanks."

"Okay, then. Be back in a jiff. Let me write down my cell number, just in case."

After Nancy left, Terri watched the car move into the icy twilight. Once it passed safely down the street, she rolled a section of newspaper tight.

Thwap. When the first one hit his chest, he bounced. Thwap. He begged, covered himself, yelled. Too. Bad. Thwap. He curled up and cried. Her jubilant yelp blended in. Thwap, thwap, thwap.

She finished right away. In her mind, beatings weren't quick.

Earl crawled from the trench. The battle banged on around him. He had to get home, his wife called. "Dinner's ready, dear," she said. "Come say grace." The succulent roast aroma drove him mad. After making his

38

way across the border, he was overjoyed to reunite with his wife and his mother. They waited at the table. Too overwhelmed to trust his emotions, he simply took his seat and began the prayer. Bless us, O Lord, for these, thy gifts...

Nancy returned to find Earl deceased. She had never known a family member to completely cover the body, with the blankets up over the head. But then, people were strange. Nancy said a prayer, she always did when a patient passed.

Terri rocked in her mother's old chair, staring out at the dark night.

* * *

Shattered

Tom's wife Marla was carrying the supper dishes to the kitchen when she collapsed and died before reaching the sink. The plates broke into pieces, as did Tom.

Now she rested on the fireplace mantel in a midnight blue urn.

The doorbell chimed but Tom didn't answer. It was probably Annette from #10-C with another lasagna and having been through it herself.

He spent Christmas lying on the couch, wrapped in Marla's afghan that still smelled of her peachy perfume. A mouse scratched behind the wall.

Mornings, he dragged in to work. Evenings, he slumped home to Marla on the mantel.

Sometimes the urn glowed from within, her essence shining through the glass.

One Saturday night, panicked with aloneness, Tom picked someone up at a bar. He rushed her past the urn to his bedroom with her coat still on. She kicked his ass with the heels of her feet and shrieked at him to fuck her harder.

Afterwards she lit a cigarette and puckered her lips, blowing smoke like kisses as Marla used to do. The cold city lights through the window colored her midnight blue. Tom's grief welled up, he turned his back to her. A mouse scampered across the bed. The woman said she had to go.

Monday, Tom woke at noon. He was still home on Wednesday. On a trip out for bread he picked up a

Shattered

hamster wheel from the pet aisle. Mice scurried freely about the apartment. That morning, he'd opened the kitchen cabinet to find a big glossy boy eating oats. They'd chewed through the box, oats littered the shelf. The mouse put its twitchy BB of a nose out at him then went back to its meal.

They wouldn't run on the wheel until he left cheese cubes on it. The wheel squeaked while he slept. His boss quit calling. Tom didn't care because he had his twenty years in and wanted to die anyway.

They'd had a child once, a premature son who lived for three hours. Tom had a half dozen hamster wheels. Sometimes he lined them up, or put them in a circle. A mouse carnival, with mouse Ferris wheels.

He bought white PVC pipes and made them a tunnel from the living room to the kitchen, to the dining room, and back to the living room.

The doorbell chimed.

"I wondered if I could get my lasagna pan?"

Annette was shapely. He went to find her pan.

She screamed.

Tom pulled a mouse out of her hair. She rushed out without a word or her pan, which annoyed him. They were only mice.

The one in her hair was Marvin. Mickey had a white spot on his back, Minnie had blonde fur, and Big Boy was huge. But Marvin dominated. He crawled over the others, snatched their food away, and humped all the girl mice.

Tom decided to return Annette's pan a couple of days later.

"Come in," she said.

Her walls were deep gold. She had lots of mirrors and plants. "Nice place."

"Thanks. Coke?"

A picture of her with a dark-haired man looked down from the bookshelf.

Shattered

She returned with his drink. He said, "You seem to be coping well."

"Ha. You should have seen me a year ago."

He went on to the grocery store with a new sliver of hope in his pocket.

When he returned, his door stood open.

"I need to speak with you," a policeman said.

He followed the officer into his apartment. Mice swarmed the floor, the sofa, the tables.

They ran in plastic mouse tunnels and on hamster wheels. Saucers of food and water were scattered about. Two other cops were present, the apartment manager, and a maintenance man, who told the woman with the camera that he'd come in on a routine roach spray and found the infestation.

Exterminators in yellow space suits brought in a big machine. "Clear the unit, please," one of them said. They spun the long attachment around and knocked Marla off the mantel.

The urn shattered on the brick hearth.

No one else seemed to notice. Tom fought a wild urge to recite "Humpty Dumpty." Brown mice wove through the particles and blue shards.

The cops huddled together, discussing him.

"Sir, encouraging vermin is a public health hazard and there's property damage involved here as well," the one who had met him in the hallway said. "I'm going to have to place you under arrest. You can sort it out with the judge." The officer handcuffed him.

Hours later, Tom was given a court date and released. He guessed he did not live at his apartment anymore, so he sat on a bench.

"Up for another round of it, neighbor?" Annette.

"Well, there doesn't seem to be any choice."

"Nope," she said. "No choice. Come on, let's get a pizza."

Shattered

Tom picked up the pieces of himself and followed her. He was glad at least that he'd thought to return her lasagna pan, and that it was made of metal.

* * *

Risen

Drifting along would be so easy. No hour of the day or night would be different from any other, no day different from the rest. I wouldn't be sure I was alive with nothing outside myself to anchor me. I'd float around my old relic-filled house like a ghost.

So I stuck with a routine, though I didn't have much reason to. The kids weren't coming for Easter, they rarely even called. I boiled a few eggs and dyed them pink with food coloring, took a thin packet of

47

sliced ham out of the freezer for my dinner. A small, foil wrapped chocolate rabbit waited on the kitchen table, glistening in the weak morning sun.

I put on my black hoodie and took my daily walk along the path in the woods. Today I cut back through the cemetery on a duty visit to Elmer. He rested in a garden crypt rather than the standard underground casket. I had bought it out of guilt and the funeral director's manipulation of my emotions. Elmer's burial cost more than his car.

Hello, Elmer. I plucked a stray weed from the base of his mausoleum, his tiny, ornately carved house. The weather's finally warming up a bit. I kept my visits with him light and surface only, like pleasant chitchat between acquaintances.

The doorknob on the little mausoleum twisted. The door creaked opened. My chest ached, as if my heart dropped into my stomach.

He emerged, stooped over, thinner and grayer than I remembered. Bruises or mold bloomed in spots on his face and hands. But, clearly, he was still Elmer.

48

"The weather's finally warming up a bit, is it? That crypt is so hot I thought I was in hell. Well, what are you gawking at, woman? Are you going to help me get home, or stare at me all day?"

Always with the questions, still. Questions from one who already knew everything. Too dizzy to protest, I held my elbow out for him to hold onto.

We trudged home through thick fog that wasn't really there.

"I'm hungry."

"All right, Elmer. Let me get another packet of ham out of the---"

"Get me a beer."

"I'm out of---"

"Why don't you get some, dammit?" He slammed his fist down on the table. The foil- wrapped rabbit bounced to the floor.

Risen

"Okay, I'm going." I rushed to the coat tree by the door, to put my hoodie back on.

"What else do you have to drink?"

"I have a bottle of Riesling in the cabinet, and some tequila, and --"

"Nevermind. Give me some wine first. Also, if it's not too goddamn much to ask, could I get some dinner around here?"

The day dragged on. Elmer ate, drank, and yelled at me. Then he watched TV, drank, and yelled at me. He stumbled to bed, and threw his shoe at me on the way.

My niggling doubt was answered, the one that had me waking up nights, out of breath. Elmer never said a word about missing me, or being glad to see me. He didn't ask if I was sad, here alone. He didn't show any sign of even liking me the slightest bit. He never said he was sorry.

Some people aren't going to change, no matter what kind of chance they get for a do-over. I guess that

went for me, too. I served him with a smile and a splash
of anti-freeze in every drink, just like last time.

* * *

The Horse Head Earrings

Venetia Favaloro's old maid sister, Luisa, was furious when her mother died in 1925 and left the horse head earrings to Venetia.

Venetia was relieved when Luisa stopped speaking to her. Venetia, with many children and few lira, lacked energy for Luisa's nattering. Venetia envisioned easier lives for her children. As her two prettiest daughters came of age, she mailed them to bridegrooms in shining America.

Upon Venetia's death in 1946, each daughter received an envelope from Sicily. Nothing fancy, just keepsakes that Venetia's own mother had left to her.

The onyx bracelet went to Antonietta in New York. The horse head earrings, to Annuzziata in St. Louis.

When Luisa heard, she had a nephew drive her, at top speed, to the village telephone. She dialed Annuzziata in America. "I command you to send me those earrings. Mamma had promised them to me," she said in Italian, crossing her fingers to excuse the bugia (fib).

"You shan't have them," Annuzziata replied.

Upon Annuzziata's death in 1968, her daughter, Carlina, moved into the house. The phone rang right away.

"I want those horse head earrings with the garnet eyes," someone warbled on the phone in broken English. "I simply must have them."

"You mayn't have them," Carlina said, having been warned that Luisa would call. "Absolutely not."

Carlina died in 1987. Carlina's daughter, Samantha, and her family, moved into the house. The phone rang as she carried boxes in.

The Horse Head Earrings

"I want those earrings," someone at the other end hissed. "I require them immediately."

"Nope. Ain't happening, Luisa." Samantha hung up.

In 2011, Samantha passed away. Her daughter, Amber, was clearing out the house when the phone rang.

"Horse head earrings," the voice croaked. "Gimme."

Amber had often repeated the horse head earring story in bars, causing everyone to howl with laughter. "Sure. Okay," she said.

A nurse named Nina got on the phone and gave the address of a rest home near Sicily. Amber wrapped them and dropped them off at the post office the next day.

Three weeks later, Nurse Nina delivered the package to Luisa. She helped her tear off the brown parcel paper. Underneath, the box was beautifully gift-wrapped and tied with bright ribbons.

"Grazie! Grazie Dio! Finalmente!" Luisa snatched the package away, and began thanking the saints individually, in between wild whoops. When she progressed to wailing and pounding her wheelchair tray, Nurse Nina had to give her a sedative. Luisa was quite frail, as expected at 146 years old.

The old woman slipped into a deep sleep and from there into the next life, clutching the colorfully covered prize.

That's what she was waiting for. The nurses agreed. After some deliberation, they decided to unwrap the package. The earrings were ugly. Enormous dangling jackass heads with embellished nostrils and seedy red eyes.

They didn't laugh until they cried yet. Not next to the body.

* * *

Turquoise Dreams

I believe most people can name their favorite color without hesitation, but I've never heard anyone say why it's their favorite. To me, it's symbolic. Turquoise blue has long-term associations in my mind with things I like.

My first crush on turquoise blue was at age seven or eight, back when girls had to wear dresses to school and the mothers usually sewed the family's clothes. We visited Grandma, who was fond of telling stories, if not in written form. She held up a beautiful turquoise-colored dress, a jumper with pleats. Grandma said a woman had come in to the fabric store where Grandma worked. The woman said she hated the store clerks and their damned fabric. She flung the dress she'd made to the floor and stormed out. The dress just happened to fit me. I don't know what to think of all that, but it soon became my favorite dress. On mornings when it was clean and ready to wear, I felt a bit uplifted, like the day ahead would be a good one. It was soft and swingy and I was a proud little peacock in my exotic dress (Peahen. Which, come to think of it, is a slightly less disgusting word than 'peacock'). The teacher said it made my eyes look turquoise blue, too.

Then Grandma's mother died. My great grandmother had left me a musical powder box. It was metallic turquoise blue and smelled heavenly, like powder. I played the melody over and over but now I don't remember what it was. I thought it impossibly grown up and sophisticated, yet she'd specially chosen me to receive it (or so Grandma said).

Also, Grandma had a large mirror with shelves on it high up on the wall. Two large ceramic turquoise

Turquoise Dreams

birds perched on the shelves, presiding over the room. The mirrored shelves themselves were magical to me, a miracle might happen in that room. I didn't understand that the mirror was just a reflection of the tiny living room. I thought it was a window into another, secret, side to Grandma's house (I may not have been as bright as advertised, as I didn't figure it out until about age ten).

Grandma herself wore a lot of turquoise blue. It went well with her coloring and white hair, which would not have been lost on her. My mom was practical, penny-pinchy and unhappy. Grandma's life was hard, but she laughed with her neighbors, played Bingo, bought me wonderful red cream sodas and treats from the Avon catalogue. She took her poodle to get its dog nails painted and matching bows on its ears. Turquoise blue was Grandma. It was snatching your smidgeon of living large when you got the chance.

I'm sure I sought out my favorite color, building on the early links between it and happiness.

Turquoise blue is the color of swimming pools, carefree summer days, the tropics, exotic vacations. I've always been a summer person.

I saved up my babysitting money forever and bought a ten-speed Schwinn bike, in gorgeous turquoise blue. I couldn't quite believe I owned it, or that I bought it myself.

Make-up, eyeshadow, stood for being almost an adult, when that seemed quite a glamorous prospect. I remember my first Maybelline eyeshadow. It was a turquoise blue.

Turquoise and silver jewelry became the big thing. It stood for rebellion, hippies, counter-culture, wildness and attitude. I adored it and stayed covered in it.

Now I'm thinking of a special turquoise colored shirt I used to have. And another.

When turquoise is offered as a color choice on a purchase, I get it. When I run across the color turquoise blue, I feel a bit uplifted.

Turquoise Dreams

Once, in a gray winter mood slump, I tried to cheer up by painting my living room vibrant turquoise blue. It made me nauseous and gave me headaches, a turquoise nightmare. Since that bad color trip, I wonder if color influences us more than we're aware of in more subtle ways as well.

The walls went back to beige, but my turquoise overdose didn't ruin the color for me. Just a dash is enough, though. As long as it's on my earrings, fingernails, necklace and shirt.

* * *

Ute Carson

texas, usa

www.utecarson.com

A writer from youth, German-born Ute Carson's first story was published in 1977. Her story "The Fall" won the Grand Prize for Prose and was published in the short story and poetry anthology, A Walk Through My Garden, Outrider Press, Chicago 2007. Her novel "Colt Tailing," was published in September 2004 and was a finalist for the Peter Taylor Book Award Prize for the Novel. Her second novel "In Transit" was published in 2008. Her poems have appeared in numerous journals and magazines here and abroad. Carson's poetry was featured on the televised Spoken Word Showcase 2009 and 2010, 2011 ChannelAustin, TX. Her poetry collection "Just a Few Feathers" was published in 2011.

An Advanced Certified Clinical Hypnotist, Ute Carson resides in Austin, TX with her husband. They have three daughters, five grandchildren, two horses and a number of cats.

The Old Should Be Explorers

The night clouds had drifted away and the morning broke silver-gray. Little had disturbed Eva and Mike's breakfast routine since their retirement from Rosewood High School three years ago. The atmosphere in the kitchen was warm and friendly and the pair sat next to each other like two content cats with their tails entwined. The water kettle whistled until Mike turned it off and poured Eva her first cup of coffee, so strong the spoon threatened to stand up.

"I need my jump-start," she said, her face bent into the vapor of the mug.

The Old Should Be Explorers

The coffee aroma was almost too much to bear as it overwhelmed the smell of fresh bagels and an alluring fragrance arising from the marmalade homemade from overripe strawberries. Eva twisted the halves of a bagel apart, handed Mike the bottom half and then began to nibble on a piece of crust from the top half. They chewed calmly while listening in companionable silence to the ten-minute news round-up on the hour.

"Joe Schreiber celebrated his 75th birthday by swimming the English Channel." The information boomed from the radio as if the announcer had performed the feat himself.

Mike ran a dreamy hand across his ample stomach, popping out of his shirt, and with a deep and earnest voice, slightly lifted, said what he always said when hearing of amazing adventures,

"Old men should be explorers."

"You've said that before, "Eva reminded him.

"No, T.S. Eliot did."

Mike pushed his chair away from the table and made his way to his study where he spent the next hours thumbing through travel guides, bent over maps and tracing his right index finger along roads and across mountains. He frowned at the volume of information until he found their next destination. A historic spot. Mike had not taught history in vain.

Eva, a fragile-boned woman who had shrunk and furrowed with age, ambled into her bountiful garden where flowers with round, sunny faces and fat heads and the odor of damp grass gave her daily sustenance. Her garden made her feel alive. Here time did not stand still. Eva used to teach photography, "time-catching" she called it. Even now she sometimes tried to capture the miracles of nature with her camera, an orange black-speckled butterfly flitting like a sunbeam from one blossom to the next or a yellow brown-spotted bug climbing the dizzying heights of a grass blade.

As the day declined, Mike and Eva retreated again to their cozy kitchen and talked over the days' events.

The Old Should Be Explorers

That evening Mike shot his long-time companion a quizzical look and let her in on his latest plan.

"We're flying to the Bahamas. *Little Exuma*, a small island. I found a deal at the *Cove Inn*. If we stay two weeks they'll throw in one extra night." Mike was always finding deals.

Mike could read Eva's reaction by the shape of her eyebrows. If she was pleased she'd draw them up into perfect arches. If she bunched them together caterpillar-style, he was out of luck. Today he got the desired response. Eva not only beautifully arched her eyebrows; she also curled her auburn, silvery-tipped hair around two fingers and said,

"Sounds great. When do we go?"

* * *

Mike and Eva were not alone in their travel zeal. Several of their friends, mostly colleagues from Rosewood High, followed the spirit of moving out and away, stepping to the tunes of a new freedom. They took to the highway in their campers with as many possessions as a vehicle could carry, each equipped with self-cleaning ovens, indoor toilets and all kinds of gadgets, connections to the familiar, the habitual, the old routine.

To get away from it all while hauling it along. Of course a few friends ventured on a one-time excursion to Europe, hitting all the major capitals in a week. But they rarely dared to dip into a foreign culture, leery of crossing untried borders. It took enough effort to reach over the fence to meet a new neighbor.

Mike and Eva and their friends had never lived rudderless lives but now was their chance to row away to foreign shores. They had done well in their jobs, generally succeeded at being good parents, and were valuable community members. As teachers they had witnessed their students' harrowing journeys from adolescence to maturity. They knew each other, had played in each others' back yards. But since retirement they shared a feeling of "now what." Suddenly there was the urge to look to the open road where they could not know what would happen around the next corner. They felt a pull to leave the nest and a longing for the whole wide world. Yet, only the calmer waters of home gave them the security of a safe haven. Damned if you do, damned if you don't!

The years of teaching had created strong bonds and the old friends often partied together. At those occasions they enjoyed the verbal bantering, the cheerful camaraderie and the high spirits that flowed from the bottle. When Mike and Eva told their friends about their latest travel plans, Susie and Jim decided to throw them a party.

The smell of charcoal-broiled meat drew Mike and Eva to the open barbecue pit.

Jim, who had taught English and was a skinny rod, popped a beer.

"Have one. " He tossed Mike a can.

His wife Susie, a foxy former biology teacher in fuchsia-red curls, rushed forward and kissed Eva on the cheek, then the air near her other one.

"Lucky you. The Bahamas. That's where I want to go."

Rita and Russ, gym teachers, were already drinking beer like water, dangling two empty cans with their fingers in the openings. They were nicknamed "the slow pokes." After retirement they had lapsed into relaxation so thoroughly that they seemed like cattle grazing on one single spot in a wide-open pasture. They needed a lot of prodding just to travel to the next town.

Max, a kind, bearded man, was there with his pleasingly plump wife, Mary, who wore billowy, flamboyant clothes to hide her girth. Both had long shelved math and science in favor of the wine rack. Drinking was Max's chosen pastime, so liquor had little effect on him. Even when he had too much, he remained as gentle and easygoing as he had been in the classroom. But as Eva always noted,

"He sure does leave a strong scent behind."

They were not all as fortunate as Max. "Drink is the downfall of many a nice girl," the saying goes. Alcohol lowers reason's guard, and what many conceal when sober, bursts forth after a few drinks. If someone was prone to sentimentality, now tears gushed forth at the sound of a sad song. Someone with a sullen disposition became downtrodden. And quarrels erupted over things that in everyday life would have been ignored. Alcohol didn't create passions that didn't exist before but it highlighted weaknesses.

Mike got puffy-faced and laughed unrestrainedly at any old joke, his whole body shaking. Lisa, another English teacher, a woman made pretty by smiling, revisited every disappointment and countless losses encountered in her life, after a few glasses of Chardonnay. Her partner Sid, nimble as a monkey on the tennis court, got heavy-boned under the influence and started sniffling when the fun ran dry.

Eva didn't remain stone-cold sober either. She liked the tipsy feeling, a certain lightness but with both feet still on the ground. She was teased by her friends for tippling champagne, as "the lady with expensive tastes."

Mike and Eva's send-off party was no different from the parties that had gone before. Alcohol kindled and inflamed the emotions.

It was several hours into the feasting when Sid sidled up to Eva, poured himself another drink, slurring his woordy words. Then he tottered across the lawn and stumbled over a wicker chair. He caught himself and called back to Eva with a whine,

"Give me a hand here. I need some help."

Both Mike and Eva scurried to his aid. They caught Sid under his arms and slung them over their shoulders for balance. Then they pulled him like a piece of driftwood, his feet dragging through the dewy grass, safely inside and onto the living room couch. There he passed out, quietly like falling asleep.

As the night darkened Jim and Susie were fairly far gone. A painfully shy man, Jim swayed, watery-eyed. He kept upright with difficulty and perspired profusely, his shirt wet as if he had taken a dip in the pool. He drooled but quickly licked the corners of his mouth. All the while Susie giggled alot.

71

The Old Should Be Explorers

Eva sauntered over to Jim, feeling a pleasant aloofness. Suddenly, quite awkwardly, Jim grabbed Eva's left arm and his fingers crawled to her wrist sluglike. His fingers lingered there as if repentant. Then suddenly he released her arm and pinched her butt. Eva winced,

"Don't do that, Jim."

But her rebuff was meek. Maybe tonight the champagne was having a paralyzing effect. Maybe she should not have worn that flimsy blouse Mike had warned her about,

"Your nipples poke through the fabric. At least wear a bra."

Eva stood, riveted to the spot. Jim belched and before she could step away brown liquid spewed from his mouth onto her yellow blouse. Jim's legs dissolved beneath him and he sank to the ground like a sack of laundry. Eva shook herself, her face a disgusted grimace.

Susie ran up and knelt down, spreading her arms over her husband like a protective coat.

Mike had had enough. He stormed toward Jim and was about to grab him by the scruff of his wet shirt when big Max intervened,

"Life is too short for squabbles. Time to head for home."

Thus ended another party with hamburgers left over for the night bugs and flies, empty wine bottles, crushed beer cans and bruised feelings. Delights and demons coiled up together.

Why did they drink? They were teachers, law-abiding citizens who would have nothing to do with the consumption of anything illegal. But alcohol was allowed and even its excesses tolerated. Why? They all had witnessed fatalities, students killed on the road, an innocent bystander run over by a drunk driver. They had listened to heartrending stories of abuse, many alcohol related. Still, they continued to drink.

The Old Should Be Explorers

"To take the edge of," Mike once said. "We all need a little escape from reality from time to time."

Mike and Eva lived in the same neighborhood as Jim and Susie and had not far to go. Their hosts stayed where they had fallen. Sid was zonked out on the couch and Max offered the remaining group a ride. Mike tried in vain to deter him,

"I know you can hold your liquor, but remember?"

Max had been stopped several times before by the lenient town cop, not for drunken driving but for signing bawdy songs which echoed from his open car windows through the sleeping streets.

"Take it easy, man. Send us a postcard from the Bahamas." Max tapped his horn twice and drove off, pitching a fit by making the gravel fly.

Eva had taken off her soiled top and was washing it in the sink when Mike ambled up from behind and wrapped his around her waist. He buried his face in her neckline and she felt his heated skin and damp hair. She let herself sink backwards against his trusted chest.

"Glad we're leaving tomorrow," she giggled.

With age Eva had become self-conscious. She avoided looking at her naked body which had given her sheer delight in her youthful years. With a mixture of awe and fear she watched her body change, her skin beginning to hang on her bones like rags on a scarecrow. She recalled her toned, willowy figure with nostalgia. Mike had never owned a willowy body and so saw fewer problems in aging.

"As long as I can get it up, I'll be fine," he assured them both.

And without waiting for Eva to dry her hands, he pulled her toward the bedroom, saying,

"Old men should be explorers."

Eva remembered when alcohol did not slow down their desire. Now she held Mike's penis in her waiting palms, wiggling and sound. But when she tried to stroke it into action, it tired and shriveled. Soon it was as small as a goldfish.

No jolts of passion traveled through Eva's body that night. The party had dulled her senses.

"We'll do it before we leave in the morning." Mike's voice sounded forcibly upbeat.

Lovers of many years, they curled their bodies around each other like two tired cats and the tension went out with the lights. Soon they snored in a hard, dreamless sleep.

It happened to all their aging friends, even the young-old. And not just under the influence of alcohol. The spell of decline had been cast and impotence was no longer a well-guarded secret. It was known that Jim and Susie ordered Viagra over the Internet. Max and Mary had long resigned themselves to separate bedrooms. Sid and Lisa were weekend lovers. And Rita and Russ were too lethargic for the joy of sex. Age was sex-friendly to only a few. And alcohol could soften the spine of even the hottest penis.

* * *

The sky did a color-changing trick from velvety purple to glossy pink. Each day Mike and Eva woke up woke up to the heartbeat of the ocean.

"Let's see where the morning takes us," was their vacation motto.

Little Exuma was idyllic. They rented bicycles and rode them to the rugged tip of the island where waves moaned with hopeless abandonment against exposed rocks. Hand-in hand they strolled along an uncluttered, dazzling white beach, and collected shells for their grandchildren. Seagulls flew loops around them and then sailed down, kissing the sea foam with the tips of their wings. On sun-baked afternoons Eva and Mike roared over the swells of the water in a powerboat. They ignored their healthy dietary resolutions and indulged in sumptuous meals in those restaurants with a welcoming atmosphere which cozied up to the sea. And they indulged in long naps, after leisurely lovemaking.

The Old Should Be Explorers

Fog rolled onto the island and clouds scuttled across the sun. Lulled by a warm, dancing breeze, Mike and Eva carried two chairs onto the porch of their cabin. A sand dune placed them out of earshot of their neighbors and the roar of the waves muffled everything but the sound of their own voices. They spread provisions from the village store onto a small stone table, a long crusty loaf of bread baked in a clay oven, juicy papayas, a variety of cheeses, and a bottle of Sauvignon Blanc. After Mike uncorked the wine, they toasted the end of another marvelous day and settled in to watching a veiled sunset. The crimson disc became glazed over by a golden mist. Slowly the evening air wrapped itself around their bodies, squeezing them into a cozy cocoon.

Eva got up and went inside to spread towels over their bed sheet and set their favorite massage oil on the night stand, a balsam of rosemary, the love charm herb.

"Making preparations for a special bedtime treat," she called to Mike.

"I'm for that."

Then Eva joined him again and asked for more wine.

"Old *women* should be explorers," she said with a fetching smile.

"Said who?"

"Says me."

She unfolded a piece of tinfoil revealing two bluish-white pills. The pill faces were inscribed with butterfly logos.

"What's that?" Mike's voice came from deep within his throat, a funeral tone.

"Ecstasy."

"Are you crazy?" Mike yelled. "Remember Whitney Houston?"

"She was arrested because she's a celebrity. I'm not celebrity."

"And I don't have the money to bail you out."

The Old Should Be Explorers

"Just an idea. Don't get all riled up."

Mike rubbed his eyes and coughed twice.

"Where did you get these?"

"My physical therapist. Try them, you'll like them, she said."

"You trust her?"

"I did my own research. But Liza uses X with rape victims."

"Rape victims!"

"Or the old and decrepit."

"The old and decrepit. Have mercy!"

"You don't have to take one."

"We have fun...always have fun...without shit like this."

"I want to explore...shit like this. You can just stand guard. I'll go ahead."

"The hell you will. Not without me."

That night woke them to another world.

A feathery, mild-mannered rain muffled the air and its wetness deepened the tone of all things. The moonlight, just a splinter like a night candle, submerged the inside of the cabin in bronze-colored mystery. The light bulbs on the night stands shone like little, unnatural suns.

Mike and Eva placed the pills on their tongues and daintily swallowed as if chewing might spoil the effect. They sprawled naked on the bed for maybe twenty minutes before adrenaline shot into their fingertips and toes and a fire raced through their veins. The light stroked across their skin lightly like scraps of lace. Their breath, sweetened with wine, mingled and their hands moved gently over each other as the pounding of their hearts filled their ears. They felt weightless, on upwards winds. Eva trembled as Mike's hot-red fingers began to knead her dewy body. Mike's face was flushed as if with fever, and sweat pored from him and mixed with the oil he began to put on them

81

both. They slithered in and over each other with the smooth grace of snakes. Several times Mike reached for the water glass. But Eva chilled and snuggled into Mike's warmth, unable to wrest her hands from him. Endlessly their tongues crawled along familiar places, dipping into crevices, hollows and indentations, marking territory in the bend of a knee, the tender elbow curve, legs spread in delight. Desire brimmed in their glassy, oddly dilated eyes, dark as blackberries. With pupils wide open, the whites around the irises glowed. They stared at each other with such rapture. It was if they were seeing each other for the first time. Their bodies were singing with ecstasy as if life itself flowed through their veins. Mike and Eva were overtaken by this passion that blossomed like a crocus in the winter of their lives.

They never reached orgasm. But it didn't matter. Their minds opened like window shades and they were attuned to each others' emotions, constantly asking,

"Does this feel good?"

"Or that?"

Mike sighed with contentment and Eva purred like a happy cat.

They were keenly aware of each other, yet they were both afloat. Not out of control---they could have reached for the phone, done what was necessary. But all hostility toward the world was gone; an oceanic feeling united them with everything and everyone. Time was an accordion. What seemed like five minutes was actually five hours. The door of the cabin gaped into an endless night and the waves crashed on shore like Wagnerian music.

What had brought them here was a longing for a perfect moment. It was granted.

Mike did not hallucinate, but Eva did. She gazed at objects and wondered,

"Am I swinging from the ceiling?"

"You are in my arms. It's the fan moving," was Mike's reassuring reply.

Mike also couldn't see the purple birds flying out of the tapestry behind the bed. And when Eva cooed,

83

"These birds are juicy grapes...plump to bursting, " Mike gripped her earlobes with his teeth and nibbled on them as if they were grapes, all the while shaking with laughter.

The next morning on *Little Exuma*, light nudged Eva and Mike awake and rays from the amber crown of a rising sun drew them from their bed and sent them running to the beach. The wet sand sucked at their feet as they stepped into the waves and waded in. The water rose above their waists, tickling their navels. They squealed with delight like little children and didn't need to be reminded that the Old *CAN* be explorers.

* * *

Photo: Sean Concannon

Tony Concannon
massachusetts, usa

85

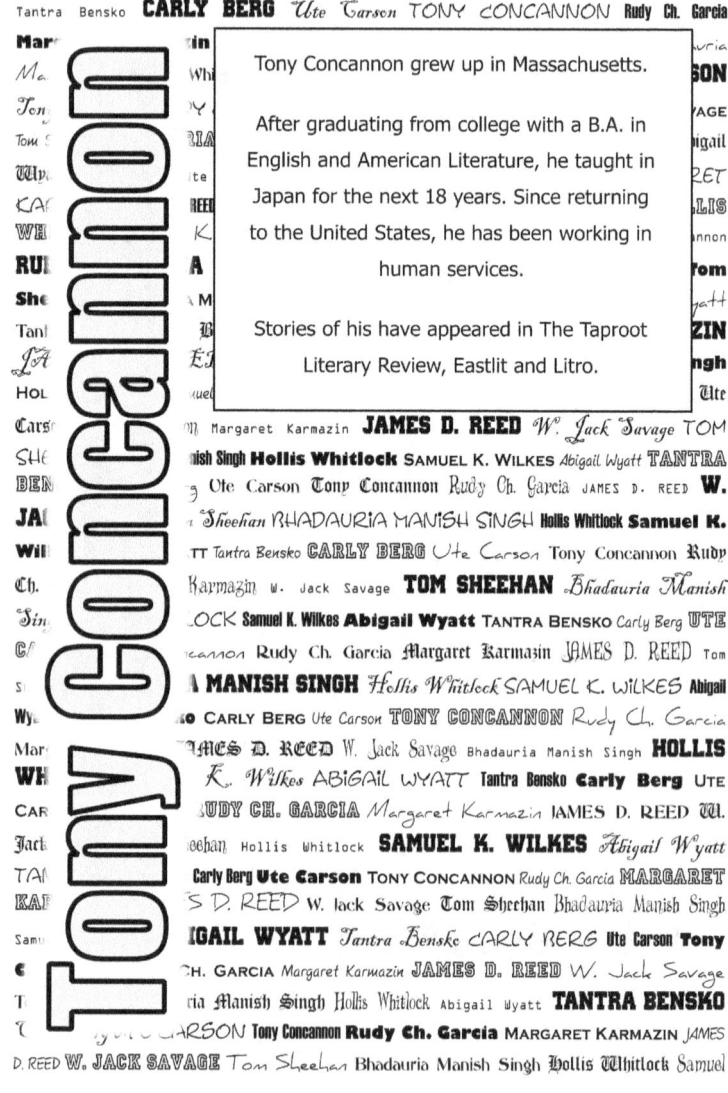

Tony Concannon grew up in Massachusetts.

After graduating from college with a B.A. in English and American Literature, he taught in Japan for the next 18 years. Since returning to the United States, he has been working in human services.

Stories of his have appeared in The Taproot Literary Review, Eastlit and Litro.

massachusetts, usa

The Book

It was snowing by the time Patrick left the library. Clutching his book, he cut through the parking lot and up Beech Street to Spruce. There was nothing to block the wind and the gusts pushed him in every direction. The lights on in the windows of the houses made it seem like evening. Karen Browne's house was further up Beech. Earlier in the day he'd walked past it on his way both to and from basketball practice. It was a big house, the largest in a neighborhood of large houses, and her father had his dental office on the first floor. Patrick's house was in the other direction, at the end of Spruce. The wet snow stung his face and blew into his mouth. Something

The Book

trickled down his back. He stopped at the crest of a hill to catch his breath. Ahead of him, in the lee of the trees, the younger boys in the neighborhood were playing street hockey. He'd played all the time until he'd started high school. Holding the book under his arm, he scooped up some snow and shaped it into a ball. From fifty feet away he lobbed it at the boys. The wind carried it into one of the yards. He made another snowball and moved closer.

"Watch out. It's Pat," one of the boys shouted.

Patrick traded snowballs with the younger boys until he was around the corner. He went up the short walk in front of his house and knocked on the door. It was a two-family house, as were most of the houses in the neighborhood, and his family rented the left side.

"You must be frozen," his mother said when she opened the door.

"I'm okay," he said, stepping into the house.

"I told you to take a hat this morning."

"It's not that cold out."

"It's going to snow all night."

"No school tomorrow."

"Oh, there won't be any school tomorrow, that's for sure."

His mother closed the door. "I made a sandwich for you for lunch," she said, going down the hall. He threw the book onto the couch in the living room and followed her.

"Don't make too much noise," she said in a soft voice. "Your father's taking a nap."

Patrick took his sandwich and a glass of milk into the living room. He settled down on the couch and opened the book he'd gotten the book at the library. He'd stopped there to look for Karen. Ever since he'd seen her studying there one afternoon, he'd looked for her there whenever he could, just as every day he walked past her house on his way to and from high school. The only other time he'd seen her outside of school had been one afternoon when she'd been helping her father wash their car in the wide driveway next to their house. Patrick had never spoken to her. It was 1971, the year of his big crush on her.

The book was a biography of one of his favorite basketball players and he was reading about the player's early life and how he had worked to become a basketball player. At two-thirty he stopped to watch a basketball game on TV. The snow was still coming down hard and he was sure there would be no school. In the middle of the game his father came down the stairs and into the living room. His unlit pipe in his mouth, he sat on the other side of the couch. He filled nearly half the couch but he wasn't fat. What was left of his hair was gray and, with his glasses on, he looked old. Patrick thought he'd aged since he'd retired from the mill in the fall. He was sixty-eight years old.

"It's really snowing out there," Patrick said.

His father took his pipe out of his mouth and looked out at the snow.

"It'll snow all night," he said.

"No school tomorrow."

His father didn't say anything. He put the pipe back into his mouth.

The weather came on when the game finished. They were predicting twelve to eighteen inches of snow. Patrick went upstairs to listen to the no school announcements on the radio. *The Sounds of Silence* by Simon and Garfunkel was being played. He opened the top drawer of his bureau and took out the picture of Karen from underneath the lining. It was his class picture from the eighth grade and she had a short, tomboyish haircut. He hadn't noticed her then. Her hair was long now, her face thinner and her chin and nose sharper. He put the picture back and stepped across the small room to the window at the foot of his bed. He pressed his face against the window and held his breath to keep the glass from fogging. The window opened onto the roof over the kitchen. Along the side of the house, where the snow couldn't reach, was a strip of bare, black shingle. Everything else was white. The snow made Karen seem far away, like a princess in a fairy tale.

He went back downstairs. His father was watching the news. Patrick took the telephone out to the hallway and closed the door behind him. The aroma of roast beef came up from the kitchen. He sat on the bottom of the stairs and dialed Karen's number, which he'd memorized from the phone book. A girl answered on the third ring and he hung up. Karen had a younger sister and he couldn't tell if it had been Karen or her sister who'd answered. He'd called before, hanging up each time as soon as someone answered. He returned the phone to the living room and went back upstairs.

He lay on the bed and listened to the radio. He could smell the potatoes roasting. The no school announcements finally came on. Only the private schools and a few towns on the North Shore had cancelled so far. He stayed there thinking about Karen until his mother called him and his father. After they'd eaten, they sat in the living room. His mother and father watched the Ed Sullivan Show. Patrick thought about Karen. No school meant he wouldn't see her until Tuesday. He picked up the book and turned the pages.

"I got this at the library today," he said to his father. Patrick held out the book to show him.

"When he was in high school, his team was playing for the state championship and he was real nervous. When they announced his name, he pulled down his sweat pants and everyone started laughing. He'd forgotten to put on his basketball shorts."

His father didn't smile.

"He scored 46 points, though, and they won the championship."

"He went through a lot of prejudice because he was black," Patrick went on. "One time, when he was driving through the South with his friends, a car full of white men started following them. When they reached the next town, they stopped. The car following them stopped, too, and the white men got out and told them they couldn't stay in the town. There was a hardware store across the street and he told them they could all go across the street and get some kitchen knives and settle who could stay in the town. The white men got back in their car and left."

His father took his pipe out of his mouth. He shook his head.

The Book

"There are a lot of wild men in the South."

He put the pipe back in his mouth. Because of his age, he'd spent the war stateside, much of it in Alabama.

"He wasn't going to let people push him around just because he was black," Patrick said.

His father took the pipe out of his mouth again.

"There are a lot of wild men in the South," he repeated.

"Things are changing," Patrick said.

His father didn't say anything. Patrick closed the book and returned it to the coffee table. His father, who hadn't learned to read until he was in his twenties, and only then because he was immigrating to the United States from Ireland, often read the books Patrick left there. Patrick stayed up late, listening to the no school announcements on the radio. School hadn't been cancelled by the time he went to bed. When he woke, the sun was shining. He sat up on the bed and looked out the window. The snow on the roof was up to the window sill. He lay back and thought about Karen. At seven o'clock he went downstairs. His mother was drinking a cup of coffee at the kitchen table.

"Oh, you can go back to bed," she said. "There is no school anywhere today."

"I will after I get my book."

"Your father's been up shoveling since six o'clock. I told him it wasn't good for his heart but he wouldn't listen."

Patrick looked out the kitchen window. The back steps and the bottom of the narrow driveway had been neatly shoveled. His father always did the driveway even though they had no car. Neither of his parents could drive.

Patrick went into the living room. The book was gone from the coffee table. He glanced out the window. The driveway was nearly finished. Then he saw his father lying in the snow.

A police car came first and then an ambulance. The ambulance driver pronounced his father dead at the scene.

"It must have been a heart attack," the ambulance driver told Patrick's mother.

"I told him not to shovel," she kept saying.

* * *

Author Rudy Ch. Garcia - tryptych self-portrait

Rudy Ch. Garcia

colorado, usa
discarded-dreams.com

Tantra Bensko **CARLY BERG** *Ute Carson* TONY CONCANNON Rudy Ch. Garcia
Margaret Karmaz

Rudy Ch. Garcia's noir detective story, LAX Confidential ('08) appeared in Bilingual Press's Latinos in Lotusland. A Southwest fantasy Memorabilia (honorable mention in a Writers Digest competition) appears in the anthologies Needles and Bones and Crossing the Path of Tellers (11/12). A fantasy flash fiction A Grain of Life: at AntiqueChildren.com ('09). Humor-fantasy-horror tale, Weird Ronnie took first place in an AlternateSpecies.com competition (Britain). The magic realism story Mr. Sumac is included in AQC Books' Kingdom Freaks and Other Divine Wonders, 7/12. A SciFi short, Last Call for Ice Cream was published by Rudy Rucker in Flurb webzine #13, 3/12. His children's fable in Spanish, El Viaje de Clarisa, appeared in Revista Iguana, 12/12. The Closet of Discarded Dreams: A Chicano fantasy novel published by Damnation Books (9/12). Book site: Discarded-Dreams.com

Garcia is a quasi-ex-member of Ed Bryant's Northern Colorado Writers Workshop, holds a B.A. in writing from CU-Denver and works as a Denver-area bilingual elementary teacher. He is a founder-contributor to LaBloga.blogspot.com, the Chicano literary website.

Author LinkedIn: Rudy.Ch.Garcia

Carly Berg UTE CARSON Tony Concannon **Rudy Ch. Garcia** MARGARET KARMAZIN JAMES
D. REED **W. JACK SAVAGE** Tom Sheehan Bhadauria Manish Singh Hollis Whitlock Samuel

Class Epiphany

Time: 5:30pm. Location: Prof. Bowen T.'s Advance Fiction class.

"We have a big schedule today! How's everybody?" booms the Anglo professor, sporting gold chains and hairstyle of his 80s TV series namesake, Mr. T.

"Sweet!" "I'm hung over, Teacher." "Tres bien, Monsieur."

"Okay, let's see who's here. Justine?"

"Present! And my critiquing pencil is extra sharp today, Profe." A couple of groans acknowledge her literary reputation, the only class member who's sold a story.

"Treber?"

"Here, Professor T."

"Natie?"

"Je suis ici, and it's Natalya, Monsieur."

"Right, Natalya. Landau... Landau? Guess he's late again... José?"

"Aquí!"

While he continues roll call, Andra whispers to Treber, a philosophy major, "That Landau: how can a guy's stories always suck and be so frackin' long? His last one about the lame art student took the curl out of my tresses." She tosses back her long, blond locks. "Only head cheese could be worse than a story written by a business major."

Half the male students follow Andra's curls, as dreamily as each one hopes to change her sexual preference.

"Andra, Honey," says a smirking Natalya, "don't knock what you never--"

"Shhhh," Treber warns, smoothing pleats in his trench coat, "entereth Mr. Laconic himself."

5:35 p.m.

Landau shoves past the heavy door, clutching folders and backpack with one arm and, with the other, hugging a box to his torso. He catches his black-rimmed glasses from slipping over his nose. Tucking his uncooperative shirttails, he steps on papers he dropped.

Mr. T says, "Thank you, Mr. Landau, for making my day."

Returning Prof. T.'s grimace with a mute "Sorry," he plops onto his desk.

Landau never planned on registering for a fiction class to fulfill graduation credits; it was beyond his meager skills. But the "good" or easy courses at CU-Denver always maxed out, and little remained after he returned from his mother's funeral.

Nobody asked why he joined the class so late--not even Prof. T--so he never mentioned the funeral. Not that it would matter to this class, most in their twenties, too young to admit death into their world. Plus, they treated him just like they trashed his prose that he labored over for days.

5:37 p.m.

Prof. T stands to the clinking accompaniment of his metal chains. "Class, on our docket today is: another no-doubt thrilling chapter about José's serial stalker. And the concluding, erotic, crime piece from Natalya that, hopefully, will not strain the loins of male critiquers. Lastly, Landau--you prepared? For the sake of our schedule, I hope..."

"I've... got another draft, Prof. T... which--"

His stammering is acknowledged by muffled: "Whoops!" "Sacre bleu!" and "He's in some deep--"

"Mr. Landau! The syllabus was meant to be as strict as the prerequisites, which, I remind you, I had to wave because you're a senior."

"Yeah--real senior," someone whispers. Snickers abound.

"Prof. T., I had a... new idea, but I'm not sure I brought--"

"Officially, Mr. Landau, you have until six-thirty, an hour from now, for your reading. Let's hope we can adhere to the schedule." Prof. T silences the metal chains against his chest. "Okay, José--you ready?"

"Of course, Bowen. My serial killer's always locked and loaded for your class."

"José Dude, how many you gonna leave dead or dismembered this time?"

"Don't worry, Treber; today, I even spared the narrator." A round of chuckling ensues.

Landau's too distracted, focused elsewhere, to share the class's mirth. He searches notebooks and

Class Epiphany

shuffles papers that came unclipped, heedless to others' smirks. Except, whenever laughter rises, he lifts his head to see if he's again the object of a brownnoser's jibe. Verbal abuse is class culture, in his case.

In fact, Landau has nearly completed his story, about an, old suffering woman, a fictionalized biography of his mother. The idea grew out of his Beginning Drawing class that he had to drop during her illness: three months from diagnosis to her cremation.

Though he never thought himself artistic--visually or otherwise--his young, art instructor seemed so sincere when praising his work, like he might have a little talent. Memories of her kind words and flashes of a portrait stream through his mind. He risks a private smile.

His art teacher's attention then inspired him to write an existential parody of aging in America, but he hadn't use those terms, since he didn't understand existentialism and struggled with the concept of parody. Aging, he did understand. But he gave up revising it when he realized Treber would expose its narrative weaknesses. And since he wasn't good at dramatic climax either, he'd also face Justine's editing wrath. The students would annihilate him.

5:50.

José wraps up his presentation. "Yeah, my closing sounds very real. I'll tell you my secret: I based it on learning how to reassemble a pump-action shotgun, to get the details right."

Everyone turns in the direction he motions--the canvas bag lying alongside Prof. T.'s desk.

"Don't worry; I got a permit from my gunsmith instructor and the ammo's still in its box. Plus, I got a note from my mom." The class chuckles, most of the males turning to view Natalya's coquettish swaying as she heads up front for her turn.

5:55.

To curry favor with his caustic classmates, Landau tinkered with incorporating their criticisms into his story, but he knew these young people would never be satisfied. He was no social butterfly, much less a a

Class Epiphany

good writer, usually an outsider, even among his generation.

He regrets that his story will never impart the passion of Natalya's every paragraph. Likewise, he can never do a presentation like the charismatic José. Any female he ever asked out on a date commented at length on the cross of moderation that he bears. So, as in the past, he knows his story will soon disappoint everyone.

6:00.

But what bothers him more is his uncompleted, final art project--a portrait of his mother, in her prime. It would have pleased the art teacher. Now, she'd never have coffee with him to give him her expert criticism, to exchange pleasantries, maybe laugh. Or lightly, accidentally, touch his hand.

"What else is left for me to miss out on?" he mumbles to himself. He reaches into the box to feel the wood-handle, art brush he yet totes around. And the other item he brought today.

From two rows over, José nods, smiling as if he noticed and understood what Landau meant only for himself.

"Did José guess? I only wish... " Landau muses, but he's out of time.

6:05.

"Mr. Landau, you haven't been paying attention. The Luck Muse isn't on your side today, since Natalya deferred anymore of her reading." Prof. T shares a quick grin with her. "So, you're up now. I assume you won't leave our dreams unfulfilled?"

Landau hadn't been sure he'd go through with it. Until something got triggered by his teacher's words. "Fulfill your dreams?" Landau pulls out the art brush, wielding it as if working a canvas.

Rising, he jams the brush into his back pocket and yells, "What about my dreams!"

Classmates freeze, perplexed. Mr. T. shoves his chair back.

Class Epiphany

"So what if I'm not funny as Treber or as good as José. So what!"

"Mr. Lan--"

"Bowen: you don't have to apologize. I'll take care of your damned schedule!" No one would need to suffer through his old-woman story.

He slams down his notebook, papers and whatnot escaping as it shuts. On his way up the aisle with the box, he shuts Justine and Treber's books, too. He clutches the hallway door handle, yanks it wide open. He turns to glare at the young does and bucks blinded by his rage. As planned, he drops the box and pulls out and cocks a 38 Smith & Wesson. He lets the door close itself and chuckles... as he changes his mind.

While he prepares to complete his final art project, the closest students who move to stop him become the first casualties. To the others, the scene unfolds like a fantasy on a wide-screen. They're stunned because though many wrote about, few ever witnessed, an epiphany.

* * *

6:45.

Through the windows, orange and blue lights flash, sirens blare as more police cars close in, their brakes screeching. Cops stand behind opened car doors, guns drawn, pointing toward the classroom. Inside, whimpers and soulful prayers from the students permeate the room. Most lay cowering on the floor.

Landau hefts José's shotgun in his left arm as he uses the brush to toss red blotches at the whiteboard, mutating Prof. T's comments into vanilla-strawberry colored drippings. Landau's revolver is tucked in his belt, but he has the class's attention.

He says to Natie, "Notice how Bowen's cooling, red corpuscles add a certain irony to the board's stark background." Landau sweeps the gold chains over his left shoulder to keep them clear and clean.

"Reminds you of the eviscerated guts from José's antagonist, no? Ha, ha! I made a funny! Don't you think so, José? Oh, that's right--Señor José can't habla with all

Class Epiphany

that lead in his mouth." As Landau rotates, the barrel's sweep makes heads duck, left and right.

"Now, Natie Dear--you don't mind me calling you Natie, right?--help me add a couple of strokes to this negative space, here... Please don't drop the brush, Love, and don't shake so; it just smears the blood. Plus, we wouldn't want to drop any on poor, dead Treber. Just step over him. That a girl! Now, Natie, let it come, real smooth. Just... so."

* * *

Margaret Karmazin

pennsylvania, usa

http://margaretkarmazin.blogspot.com/

Margaret Karmazin has had over a hundred short stories published by American, Canadian, British and Australian literary and sci-fi magazines. Four of her stories have been nominated for Pushcart awards and one for the 2010 Million Writers Award. Her young adult novel Replacing Fiona and children's picture book, Flick-Flick and Dreamer, were published by etreasurespublishing.com.

She is also an artist with illustrations and paintings published by SageWoman and several American literary magazines.

He'll Do

Hard to believe that thirty years earlier, they rode Harleys, partied all night and made love for entire weekends, ignoring the ringing phone and friends pounding on the door. He became her third husband, the one that "took" after a disastrous two divorces. Like everyone, Gina had imagined this exuberance would go on indefinitely, but as happens to anyone who lives long enough, she ran into the brick wall of time.

She was there with Roy at the doctor's when he gave them what she immediately knew was going to turn out a death sentence: "I'm afraid the biopsy came back positive, Roy. I'm giving you the names of three oncologists and you can-"

He'll Do

Gina interrupted. "Can't you just pick one and set up the appointment for us, as soon as possible?" She wanted to get started on the treatment; maybe Roy would stand a chance if they just got started.

"Of course," said the doctor.

Outside in the damp cold, Roy looked like he had aged ten years. "You should have given us time to check out the three doctors."

She could hardly hear him. In her mind's eye, in front of his face, their life together was rushing past, from start to...to...was this the finish? Of course it was. What had she expected, forever? He was ten years older than her; she should have known this was coming.

She grabbed hard on his sleeve. "I love you so much, Roy, I love you so much. Please, Roy, don't leave me. This world sucks, it's only bearable with you in it."

He put his long arm around her and pulled her close. Around them snow swirled, those big fat flakes that disappear when they hit the ground.

"I'm being selfish," she said. "All that matters is how you feel right now, not me."

The dreaded appointment had been made, for only three days hence.

"Let's go have double cheese pizza," Roy said. He had not been allowed to have such things because of his cholesterol, but now what the hell.

"I don't think I can eat, Hon," she said. "Let's just get one and take it home."

After that, everything passed in a whirl of hand wringing, fear and pain. Eight months later, Roy was gone. She drugged herself through the funeral and the months after while she dealt with medical bills, removing his name from accounts and cars, and trying to placate his children from his first marriage who suddenly accused her of stealing their inheritance. What a laugh. Roy, who had never earned as much as she, had about ten thousand dollars to spare, that was it. She divided it among the children and closed the books.

He'll Do

The house was screamingly empty and suddenly there was nothing to do. For months she had been Roy's nurse and at the end when he was in the hospital, by his side day and night. Now she had no purpose, no reason at all to get up, yet she could not sleep.

"You're a mass of tension," said her chiropractor as he worked her shoulders. He handed her a pillow and told her to hug it and exhale while he did a side maneuver. She heard the crunch.

"Yeah," she said, "I think my fibromyalgia is back."

"How are you doing?" he asked when they were done, his eyes giant and blue behind his glasses.

Her eyes filled up, probably the fortieth time that day. Unable to get her voice to work, she shook her head.

Laurent, who was French Canadian, laid his warm hand on her shoulder. He had a slight accent, which usually soothed her, but now nothing seemed to.

"I cannot imagine what you are going through. If anything happened to Lisa..." He didn't finish.

"This is how it all ends, Laurent. Starts out good, turns to shit."

"You need some serious work," he said, ignoring that last statement. "A massage might help you loosen up. I can recommend-"

"I know a masseuse," she said without interest. What she'd do instead was go home, swallow another Xanax and sit for hours in her recliner, sobbing her eyes out while she watched Home & Garden. The cat would lie on her chest and purr, but she'd feel no pleasure from it, none at all.

Everyone was kind. Her daughter Christie tiptoed in and out of the house, straightening up the kitchen as she passed through, taking towels to the washing machine, asking what Gina might need from the store. Friends and acquaintances showed up, toting wine, containers of homemade soup, tuna casserole, macaroni and cheese. Neighbors shoveled the driveway, carried her garbage cans to the curb, came running

He'll Do

when her Jeep needed a jump, when the garage door refused to open, when her internet crashed, not that she spent much time on the computer. What for? What was anything for?

"I brought you some books," said Christie, setting a stack on the coffee table.

But Gina could not read. She would stare at a page and the little black squiggles refused to form into words. Or if they did, the words made no sense.

Before Roy passed, they'd slept in separate bedrooms, Roy in the one just off the living room and Gina upstairs. After his massive heart attack seven years before and his ever present aortic aneurism, he was afraid that sex would finish him off, which indeed it might have. He was a big man and took up a lot of the bed, so gradually they had changed their sleeping arrangements. Now his room lay empty. She could not bring herself to use it, though it would have been more convenient. She rarely slept now in her own room for that matter, choosing instead to pass the endless nights on the sofa.

One evening about two months after his death, Gina heard him call out from the bedroom. "Gina!" he said, loud and clear in that voice like no other.

She was shaken, but happy. After a pause, she got up from her chair, knocking the cat to the floor and several unread catalogs. She crept toward the bedroom, knowing full well that no one would be there, but irresistibly drawn.

Of course, the room was empty, but where had that voice come from? She'd been completely awake, about to pick up the remote control to change the channel, thinking about getting herself something to eat. Of course she would love to hear this voice, but she'd certainly not been thinking about it at the time. What did it mean?

She told a friend what happened.

The friend, Eleanor, did not find it unusual. "I've heard many reports of people seeing or hearing their passed on loved ones," she said. "Either it was an audio hallucination caused by your subconscious or it really was Roy's voice calling to you. I don't know."

He'll Do

It never happened again. Nor did she see Roy standing at the end of her bed, once she had returned to her bedroom to sleep, nor later when she began to use his bedroom. But she never forgot the sound of that call with the exact essence of his voice all those years she had loved him.

She flew to Prague, Barcelona and Hawaii with old classmates, Ireland and Netherlands with former work mates. She bought diamond earrings, garnet bracelets, silver charms and got a tattoo on her ankle. She ordered new jeans and tops and dresses, but the house was empty, no matter how many new objects came into it. No matter what friends stopped over or how many called. No matter that almost two years had passed.

"We're having a cookout," said her former coworker Leigh.

They'd met for lunch at Olive Garden where Gina was rather desperately sucking on a straw embedded in a tall Bloody Mary.

"Uh huh," she said, picturing another tedious social event where she was expected to "act normal" though the entire rug of life had been yanked out from under her.

"Labor Day weekend, Saturday, three o'clock, BYOB if you want something other than wine and beer. Don't worry about food, we've got that covered."

Racking her brain for an excuse to decline, Gina sipped harder.

"Don't try to get out of it," said Leigh. "You're coming, period, the end."

"All right," Gina mumbled as she sucked noisily at the bottom of her glass. Damn.

His name was Vic and he was a friend of Leigh's brother-in-law Mark; they had known each other for a long time, both being in the building trade, Mark an electrician and Vic a contractor. Now retired, Vic lived in a neatly maintained split level home with his two bird hunting dogs, Whistle and Snap. The dogs were pedigree, smart and obedient. He ran a tight ship.

He'll Do

There was something about his mannerisms and the turn of his words that reminded her of Roy, though the two men looked nothing alike. Roy had been tall and thin, while Vic was average height and muscular with a slight pot belly. He had smallish hands while Roy's fingers had resembled those of a concert pianist. She was not attracted to Vic physically, having always preferred tall men. Her husband's eyes had been dark, which had always given her a little thrill, the way they could look right through you. Vic's eyes were gray. He was seventy years old, three years older than herself.

"You see how good a shape he's in," Leigh said the next day when she called to pick Gina's brain. "He has his own workout machines. He could probably beat up the average forty year old, maybe even thirty."

"An admirable trait," said Gina semi-sarcastically.

Actually, it was a pretty nice thing, though she imagined he would still look grizzly and old with his clothes off. Though who was she to talk? She was thirty pounds overweight. Roy had loved her body; it didn't matter what the scale said, he had told frequently that she was beautiful. She had walked around naked in front of him, never embarrassed. Once again, her eyes filled up.

"You know he's comfortable financially. I don't mean rich, but he's taken good care of things that way."

"What's the deal with him and women?" asked Gina, though she didn't want to give Leigh the impression she was all that interested. "Is he widowed, divorced, what?"

"Divorced. Twice. I know that's a red light, and I don't know all the circumstances, but Mark says Vic is good people and Mark usually knows."

"If he tells me his ex-wives were crazy, I will bolt, " said Gina. "I am always suspicious when a man says that because later you usually learn he is a jerk and that's why the women freaked out. "

"Well, sometimes people actually are crazy," said Leigh.

He'll Do

That evening Vic called to ask her out. "Dinner, lunch, breakfast, whatever you like," he said. Had he gotten her number from Leigh? Apparently.

She didn't really want any part of this, having already decided that she would simply enjoy what time she had left hiding out in her own little world with her books (by now she could read again), movies and cat and doing the occasional trip or lunch with friends, mostly widowed like herself. What did she want a man for? She sure wasn't planning on letting anyone get sexually intimate! The thought of that made her shiver with distaste.

Should she just nip this in the bud right now? "Lunch," she heard herself say. "Lunch is best. I've got a lot to do."

"Well, don't we all," he laughed. He set the time and place since she did not want to be picked up; a well known Greek diner on Rt. 1. Not fancy, but comfortable and the food was good.

They hit it off in several ways, but in one major area they did not. "I'm a Liberal," she told him, annoyed at a remark he'd made about Hilary Clinton.

"I'll straighten you out," he said, chuckling. That irked her even more. She hated over-familiarity and more than that, right-wingers.

But what she did like, and greatly miss, was good-natured affection, even if she had consciously decided against it. It had been a long time since she'd had any.

Their lunch consisted of thick, New England clam chowder and Greek salads. Vic was concerned with his health, firm about eating his veggies and had encouraged her to order the salad. "I'll cook for you the next time we get together," he told her. "How about Friday evening?"

She sighed as she drove to his place that night. What was she getting herself into? At this point in her life, she had things the way she wanted them, minus of course Roy. Her income consisted of a pension from forty-three years of teaching elementary school plus

He'll Do

Social Security, and came to more than what she'd made when working. Her house and car were paid off. She preferred things the way she had them arranged in her house, her knickknacks, pictures on the walls, furniture arrangement, her *stuff*. She liked to watch the TV shows she wanted, not to sit there bored stiff while enduring someone else's choices and she could tell right off that Vic was not going to want to see Home & Garden, nor Dancing With The Stars.

As she had explained to Leigh on her cell as she was getting dressed for this dinner, "How much time do I have left, for crying out loud? I certainly don't plan on spending any of it watching How To Hunt Moose or something tedious like that!"

"I don't think he hunts moose," Leigh said.

He was cooking when she got there; the aromas emanating from the kitchen distracting. He served fresh trout, Middle Eastern rice, buttered carrots and a romaine salad with vinaigrette dressing. No dessert. White wine of some kind. Was he going to try to seduce her after?

He didn't. Instead he told her about his hip replacement. "I might have to have the other one done. I'm looking forward to that about as much as Marie Antoinette looked forward to the guillotine."

She liked him for that analogy or whatever it was. Maybe he didn't hate France like every other reactionary she knew. He did kiss her at the door when she was leaving. She had stayed until nine-thirty; her bedtime was around ten-thirty and she had to drive home.

"No one thinks about stuff like hip replacements when they're young," she reported to Leigh the next morning. "Back then we had energy to burn, we'd stay up up night, just sleep late the next day to recover." She had to stop talking because Roy came to mind, those nights they spent smoking dope, talking about everything, making funky love.

"Are you still there?" asked Leigh.

"I was just....I was just thinking about Roy."

He'll Do

"Try not to compare them. They're nothing alike. Think of it this way: you have different friends and you don't expect any of them to be like any of the others. One doesn't replace another one, they're just different."

"Yeah," said Gina quietly, her voice tiny and lonely. "Maybe it's better not to have anyone at all rather than someone who is not Roy."

"Well life is hard," said Leigh, "and the road is lonely. Sometimes you gotta see that side of it."

Well, Leigh still had the love of her life and Gina did not, so easy for her to philosophize. She went to bed that night, torn up inside. Off and on sobbing about Roy and every few minutes experiencing a war between what she felt like doing, which was just being home by herself with her pain and what she thought she *should* be doing. She felt this *pressure* to "get on with her life," something she'd heard people say, whatever the crap that actually meant. What life? Wasn't she just putting in time, trying to entertain herself until she could lie down and expel that last breath?

What would Christie say if her mother got herself a boyfriend? And it *would* just be a boyfriend, that's it. No way was she going to do laundry, cook for and clean up after a man again, certainly not one she did not love, not even if she eventually did! And what if she got involved and he went and died on her? How could she bear to go through that again?

What would Roy say about all this? Though he was silent, no calling her name now when she could actually use the help, she did feel a sort of sudden peace around her. As if Roy was amused.

"I haven't gotten laid for what?" Vic said. "Way over a year. So don't expect much." He was jokey, but his eyes showed the real story. This was six weeks after they'd started "dating," which Gina supposed was what you'd call it. A few dinners out and he took her fishing, taught her how to cast. He invited her to social gatherings at his hunting club. He was an outdoors type of man, unlike Roy who, when not working, preferred the indoors as she herself did - cozy with her magazines and movies, afghan and telephone.

He'll Do

Now they were having sex and it was good. She had to admit, maybe even better than it had been with Roy, back when they'd done it. Vic had excellent technique, could play her like a musical instrument. He must have had many lovers, but then she herself had been around some too. Glowing afterwards, back home in her own bed, she felt rejuvenated, as if she had received a giant B-12 shot. He'd "cleaned her pipes," that was for sure. It amazed her how juicy and ready she'd been, old broad that she was.

Vic did not approve of any television show that promoted Liberalism or anything that went against his literal interpretation of the Bible. He watched FOX news.

"You know," she told him, "FOX has been caught in numerous lies. They don't seem to go for actual facts on there."

He went off on a spiel that she pretended to listen to; she'd heard/read it all before, blah blah blah. Leigh had emailed her scientific studies showing by MRI, etc. that the brains of conservatives were constructed differently than those of liberals, so no matter what you say, no liberal is going to convert a conservative and vice versa. Apparently, conservatives had a much larger fear area of the brain which probably explained why they were always poised like guard dogs to fight anything foreign or what they call "socialist." While liberals had more confidence about exploring new and exotic territories, hence their being sympathetic to things exotic or new.

When she told Leigh how Vic was politically and religious-wise, Leigh grew sarcastic. "Puke. I figured he was somewhat conservative, what with the hunting and all," she said, "but I didn't know how far right he does swing. If I'd known that..."

"I'm glad I met him," Gina burst in. "Even so."

"Are you in love?" asked Leigh, her voice radiating disapproval.

Why was she now so negative when it was she who had introduced Gina to Vic in the first place? It seemed to Gina that half the time, people were totally unreasonable.

He'll Do

"He's a good man," she said, hackles up.

"Well, better you than me," said Leigh. "I wouldn't be able to overlook that stuff, you know how I am."

Christie was the same. Election time came and went, but she was still ranting about Vic's obvious choices at the polls. "He's gotta be plain stupid," she told her mother. They were in Gina's kitchen where Christie had settled down after work for a cold beer. "Anyone that believes that literal Bible crap and can support candidates who want to take away our reproductive rights can't be the sharpest knife in the drawer! I don't know how you can sell out like this. I'll tell you this, Mom, don't bring him over to our house - I don't want to hear his political garbage. Rick won't stand for it either."

Gina felt a sudden urge to slap her. "You're forty years old! You have Rick who loves the crap out of you. You've got your figure, your health, maybe fifty more years ahead of you! Who are you to tell me what to do? That I should live without affection or companionship because maybe I don't agree with the man on every little issue! Wait till you're my age - what've I got? Twenty more years at the most? Probably the last ten of those a physical wreck? Get off your high horse and leave me be!"

Christie sighed, finished her beer and stood up. "Maybe you're right. I guess I just miss Roy."

Once she was out the door, what Christie had said kicked Gina in the stomach. Out came the picture albums, which she mulled over till she cried herself to sleep. The phone rang several times, but she ignored it. The last thing she wanted was to talk to Vic. He seemed a pathetic substitute for what she saw in the photos, years of loving, things that were impossible to replicate. Besides, though she'd never admit it to Christie or Leigh, he did get on her nerves with his caveman beliefs. So what if the sex was decent?

But when Vic called the next morning, all riled up and worried that something had happened to her, she softened, let his comforting voice soothe her, told him she'd been all sad about Roy again and he was kind.

He'll Do

"I know, honey," he said. "From what you and other people tell me, he was a good man all right. I don't expect you to forget him."

How kind, she thought. Not an ounce of jealousy, just understanding. That night he made her Beef Wellington and then fired her up on all cylinders. He must have taken a larger dose of Viagra.

"Why do you have to go to *his* house all the time?" asked Eleanor, whom she hadn't talked to in over a month. They'd met for lunch at Red Lobster.

Outside the window, spring was popping out in tiny green buds and sweet bird tweets. "Actually, I like it that way," she said. "I go there around five o'clock, he makes dinner, I help him clean up, we play with the dogs then watch some TV. If I want to see my own shows, I go in the bedroom while he stays in the living room. If we're going to 'have a date,' he comes in and we get busy. I doze off a little, then get up around nine-thirty or ten and come home. Then I relax a bit with the cat, maybe chat on the phone with somebody, before hitting the sack."

"This is every evening?" said Eleanor as the waitress set down their plates.

"Pretty much," said Gina, digging in. "I keep Monday nights for myself. Sometimes other nights. I really don't want him coming into my territory and trying to change things."

Eleanor nodded. "I getcha," she said.

Both Gina and Vic endured a few health issues. He had the second hip replacement and she nursed him for weeks. She needed some cardiac tests and a colonoscopy, which Vic drove her back and forth from. She helped him redecorate his living room and bedroom, he took care of her Jeep after its transmission conked and when her toilet backed up, he was there in a jiffy brandishing a plumber's snake.

If she had to listen to right-wing spiels, it was a small price to pay. When he quoted the Bible about gays, she refrained from pointing out that if you were going to obey what the Old Testament said, you'd sell your daughter into slavery, stone a person for adultery and execute them for working on the Sabbath. Life, she figured, was a constant compromise.

"What do you say we take a trip out West?" Vic said that evening over dinner. He served homemade split pea soup with chunks of ham in it and slabs of multigrain bread smeared with butter. "See Yellowstone Park, Mount Rushmore, some of those old ghost towns they fixed up, do the tour. What do you say?"

She would rather do Paris, London or Rome, but remembered her dad telling her once, "Never turn down a chance to travel."

"Sure, why not?" she said between spoonfuls of the thick soup.

He wasn't Roy, not anywhere close, but he was Vic and she was going on with life.

* * *

James D. Reed

ohio, usa

James D. Reed is a freelance graphic artist and copywriter with previously published stories in The Nebraska Review, Perceptions, The Feathered Flounder and Midwestern Gothic, among others.

He and his wife live on a farm near Hamilton, Ohio.

138

Just One More Thing (To Go Wrong)

1.

From his trailer up to the small Ohio college town was about nine miles if he went by way of the two-lane state route where the dysfunctional kids liked to hug your ass tailgating, hoping for a chance to veer off into the breakdown lane, and then pass you on the right, spitting giggles and flipping the bird—and cut back in as tight in front as they'd just been behind.

Or a couple miles farther if he drove the township pike where the scenery was more pleasing and his anxiety downloads less frequent.

He took the township route this evening, under a sagging, cloud-soaked sky that since afternoon had teased rain but so far had no intention of putting out.

Just One More Thing (To Go Wrong)

The stroboscopic effect of red and iridescent blue pulses throbbed eerily through the undercarriage of the cloud mass, reflected upwards from somewhere ahead. Or, he thought, an hallucination: the squirrel inside his brain gnawing rabidly at his retinae, desperate for escape from its whirling treadmill.

Around the next bend, the source: a sheriff's cruiser barricading both lanes, emergency flashers piercing the air. Behind it, two more cruisers, a squad car from New Bastion, the township EMT ambulance and hook-and-ladder truck—all orchestrated in the symphonic light show.

A beefy deputy approached, catcher-mitt hands above his head, punching the air as if trying to push Hub back even though he had already come to a complete, obedient, stop.

"May as well turn around, bud. We're locking the scene down. It's gonna be all night before we're out of here,"

In the yard of the small cinder block house where all the vehicles had converged were more deputies, helmeted and wearing armored vests, several armed with assault rifles, all milling around in groups of twos and threes, their work obviously completed. One was stringing yellow tape around the perimeter of the house and across the driveway. He paused to lift the ribbon for the EMTs who had carried something off the front porch. They wheeled a cot across the humpy, unmowed lawn, jostling its cargo, a paisley-emblazoned body bag.

"What the hell happened here?"

"Not quite sure yet." The deputy cocked his jaw, eyed the EMTs loading the body bag into the ambulance. Nonchalant, acerbic. Hub thought the cop most likely had witnessed scenes like this a hundred times and then went home to a steak dinner and an evening of watching *Law and Order* re-runs. "Guy holding his own goddamn family hostage. Who knows why. Give 'em any reason. Just as we about talked him into coming out unarmed, he steps onto the porch eating his shotgun barrel. And kaboom."

"Jesus. Shot himself?"

Just One More Thing (To Go Wrong)

"Well, *yeah*. SWAT boys didn't even have to go in. Wife and kids ran out right behind him, little boy puked his guts out on top of his old man. They're in a car over there with the grief counselor. He always tags along—you know—just in case."

"Lucky bastard," Hub mumbled.

"What?"

"Nothing." Wondering, as he backed up, if that quick, sure way was worthy of consideration. As painless.

On the streets of New Bastion he passed coeds probably no older than his own daughter—and who had gone to live with his brother Everett since he was the only family left after the accident who Family Services ruled could take care of her. The accident itself another tragedy unknown to Hub during his years of self-exile, living out of a '68 batwing door VW Kombi he'd cobbled into a camper. Coleman block-ice cooler, camp stove, somebody's tossed out deck chaise. Avoiding the alcohol fueled rowdiness, the screaming brats, the nasty, eternally yapping mutts of public campgrounds, Hub slept most nights in the relative anonymity and safety of church parking lots.

So Hub, purposely lost somewhere along the blue highways of the hinterlands in the sputtering Kombi, hired on to just enough odd-jobs here and there to sustain a high-carb, junk food diet and buy enough gasoline to keep mobile. Stayed around until people wanted to get friendly, to talk about themselves, to ask conversational questions about his life, which he viewed as so messed up it was neither any of their business nor worth describing. He didn't learn about the accident, the deaths, the custodial situation of his daughter, his brain-injured mother in a nursing home—until a couple years afterward when he decided to surface in his hometown of New Bastion, the VW broke down and him as well, having piss problems, stage 2 diabetes, blood pressure through the roof, with kidneys about as useless as tits on a tree stump. And just a few hundred bucks wadded into a roll in his jeans pocket.

The college girls were so far out of his league they didn't interest him much anymore. Rich snots with no brains. Half-naked butts in tight jogging shorts,

Just One More Thing (To Go Wrong)

sweat-spotted sports bras, jouncing down the sidewalks. The few times he went into one of the local stores or junk food carry-outs and they caught him taking an innocent peek he got eyeballed back for what they saw: a frizzy-faced hick with a wild patch of straw colored hair extruded from the back of his sun-bleached ball cap like an uprooted wad of weed-killed crabgrass. Bandy legs pushed into patch-kneed jeans the color and sheen of aluminum foil. Eyes like steel ball bearings lodged into the 100 point pay-off sockets of a pinner machine—screwed into scrimshaw creases etched deep by too much solar exposure and life-long squinting against nearly everything in front of him that never once made any predictable sense.

After he crawled back to New Bastion—even before he resigned himself that something was not right in his abused body and sought out a cheap town doc who might accept half payment cash for the exam—he looked for work. The old hardware store where his father had started the business that eventually brought him wealth was a logical choice.

Sam Spite, behind the cluttered counter, in freshly starched bib overalls that corresponded ridiculously with his tobacco-smeared grin, barely remembered Hub, looked askance at his ratty costume, the weeks-old beard growth. Informed that he wasn't hiring now or any time soon.

"Sorry to hear about the old man, though," Spite added almost as an aside while he rang up an impatient customer whose credit card had just been denied. "Have you gone seen your Mom yet?"

Hub felt like he, too, had suddenly been side-swiped against the blind side of a speeding semi by a hit-and-run driver when Spite filled out the details of the Florida smash-up on I-10 that took out his father, Hub's ex-wife, spared his daughter Holly, and sent his mother and five passengers of the other vehicle to Madison County Memorial Hospital where two of those five were DOA. The Hardtaks had been on their way to Tallahhasee where Everett Sr. planned to retire and sign over the newly formed franchise home improvement business to his eldest son. Hub had no idea his mother was now in the New Bastion nursing home. Nearly

Just One More Thing (To Go Wrong)

knocked over a display of seed packets on his way out the door of Spite's store.

He put down the first month's rent on a trailer out in the boonies shoved up against a fifty acre crop field in return for fixing up the ruined thing, keeping the pipes thawed in winter, driving raccoons out from entrance holes underneath. While the owner immediately left town for the greener pastures of New Mexico, the plan there to cultivate medical marijuana and maybe open a combo high-test weed dispensary/baked goods emporium, strike it rich and legit with the western dopers. But to Hub the guy was geared up to be a perpetual loser and during the months he lived in the trailer Hub worried the thing would be foreclosed on, or sold out from under him in the likely event the absentee landlord suddenly needed bail money—or the cost of a coffin after an altercation with Mexican outlaws.

Hub made visits to the hardware store—even though Spite had laughed at the application—went there to rent tools, buy nails, plywood, plumbing fixtures that he could not seem to master for the constant upkeep of the trashed-out, rented trailer. Pipes cracked, floor rotten where the sink leaked out. The thing threatened to list off its fractured cinder block trapeze every time a good wind tore across the tops of the soybeans.

Then he got the news that his kidneys were nearly shot. And—three fist-clenched times a week— went to the New Bastion DaVita clinic to get his oil and filter changed. A hated routine, tubed to the dialysis machine with nothing else to do but endure the ennui, the leg cramping four hour treatment, go home, skip a day and then return. A routine he frequently ignored in spite of warnings by his nephrologist. He had found that Medicare would pay for it all.

Hub managed to trade in the VW for an old F-150, spidered with cobwebs of rust, and with a rattling front fender somehow attuned to the speedometer, that vibrated spasmodically at precisely twenty-eight miles per hour. He duck-taped a piece of coat hanger wire to the antenna stump, the radio reception crackly, but better than none at all. And repurposed the old eight-track from the VW into the pickup's dash.

Just One More Thing (To Go Wrong)

Hub got a mongrel tabby from the local pound, named it EmmyLou after the singer whose old tapes still worked in the deck. Had most of Harris's early albums and the duets with Parsons, Ahern, Dolly, Linda Ronstadt, plus a rare one backed up by Chris Hillman.

The cat was precious to him, gave unconditional affection in return. Always underfoot, rubbing, twisting, turning figure 8's around his ankles whenever he entered the trailer—as if she wanted to tumble Hub to the floor, bring him down to her level so she could nuzzle close, lick his nose, get the motor going. She was like a puppy he could summon from one end of the trailer to the other with only a soft whistle. When he was propped up in the ratty, courtesy-of-Goodwill recliner, EmmyLou would hurl herself into his lap, twist, turn, mash down the virtual grasses, find the perfect burrowing spot, warm, safe, submit to cheek pets and the favorite kneading of the rubbery skin of her neck. Got the motor going loud.

The cat and his mother were Hub's only living possessions. And Mo's tucked away from reality in the back corner of an Alzheimer's unit nine miles up the pike. Sometimes she's aware of him, other times not; the old widow is not blind, yet Hub imagines she chooses to see other people—friends from her youth, relatives long faded into granite inscriptions—when he stands before her in that claustrophobic room.

When it's Hub she recognizes he catches a glimmer in her eyes like distant heat lightning over the horizon on an evening of flashing, pendulous clouds. Clouds that look like a painter has taken sable loaded with chromium green and swished it over soaked water color paper. Her irises are that color, the twitch of lightning is recognition that fades as the clouds fold together and the paint dries in its wash.

He goes to be with her every day, even though. After the dialysis sessions, and on the days off the nightmarish machine. Puts down a fresh bowl of water and a saucer of EmmyLou's favorite crunchies. Drives up and checks in on Mo. Who may or may not recognize him this particular time around.

Hub's brother, Everett B. Hardtak II, seven years older, slope-shouldered, size 16 ½ EEE shoes that Hub had, in their youth, relentlessly teased him were like whaling boats, took after Mo, their mother. Both were over six foot tall, and Everett, at the age of fifteen, sprouted another four inches into adulthood whereas Hub and Everett Sr. were all under five-six. Ev Sr., his shallow chest level with the old hardware store counter, was runty enough to have acquired the nickname "Stump" that stayed with him all the way through the wealth that awaited him as the franchise business fanned out over Ohio and four neighboring states and eventually three stores in central Florida.

After the accident, Everett II took over the franchise operations which had, directed by their father's will, been put in Mo's name along with a substantial trust fund that named his eldest son as trustee. When the will had been taken out, no one ever suspected that Mo would be incapacitated by an intracranial hemorrhage, so Everett II (who had been on a Caribbean cruise with two lady friends at the time of the accident) promptly finagled himself as power of attorney over his mother's affairs.

Everett was clueless about handling a business, having perennially lived off his father's investment incomes and monthly handouts. He was always expected to just stay the hell out of sight. He moved to Tallahhasee with his niece after the funerals when no one could locate the wandering Hub, gone God knew where after the divorce and a rattling breakdown that landed him for months in a rehab center. Hub hit the road after he cleared his head of the image of his wife humping his best friend on the dining room table, middle of an afternoon, Hub coming home early with a surprise bouquet of romantic one dozen red carnations.

Arrived in the trailer's battered mailbox a square envelope of heavy laid, buff paper with the flowery initial **H** embossed in purple ink on the flap over the upscale address, in equally ornate script, of Killearn Point Trails, Tallahhasee, Florida.

Hub slit open the envelope and unfolded the thick stationery.

Hulbert:

Just One More Thing (To Go Wrong)

On the off-chance you might still be alive I called information for New Bastion and got "no such person listed...could it be under another name, sir?" Hell no. So I got your address thru the nursing home where they have you listed as "in case of emergency". Which struck me as odd since you don't have even a cell phone.

Anyway, since it has been a long time—years— since you disappeared and none of us had a notion how to get in contact, I figured it was time to try and reach you. And sorry if it's bad news.

I've hired a lawyer to help me sort out my situation and that of Holly's. The business has gone to hell. Two of the stores down here are sitting empty in abandoned malls because of stiff competition from the likes of Lowes and Home Depot, and the rest. I can't supply the other franchises and there are now lawsuits. I'm going to have to go into receivership or Chapter 13 or something. I simply don't understand this crap. The lawyer talk is over anyone's head.

I've had to sell most of the stock which is about worthless anyway and clean out the trust to help rescue all this and still keep me and your daughter from living out of a cardboard box beneath an overpass and eating dog food. Ha ha.

You never knew it because you never called, but Holly has suffered big-time from diabetes for years and is nearly blind and now has become pregnant and is so overweight she was too far along before she realized it. It was too late for an abortion and no Daddy has surfaced to claim the prize. She's due in about 2 months.

I don't know how I can keep paying for the nursing home. The lawyer advised I can take anything left over (after the lawsuits) out of Mo's name and put it in mine and then Mo goes on Medicaid. He says I can by-pass the 5 year look-back laws because of Holly's blindness if I claim her as a dependant. It's all too damn complicated to spell out here. Lawyerese, Social Security rules and all. Too much to write about.

Just One More Thing (To Go Wrong)

After I had Mo admitted I deposited some cash into what they called a "Sunny Day Fund" to pay for extra expenses (sometimes they take the old codgers out for entertainment, restaurants, etc.) I figured about $1000 would take care of it.

The nursing home person says you visit Mo regularly on a daily basis and I'm honestly grateful for that. I guess you made up for being so worthless all those years that even Dad thought you weren't going to amount to much, that it wasn't your fault, he thought you might have been born retarded.

No, you're doing the right thing now and apparently the worm has turned and I haven't. If you have got religion as you righted yourself, pray for me and Holly and your grandchild about to come.

—Sincerely, Ev

Hub secures his pants belt against a block of wood on the yard-sale supplied kitchen table. He's bargained with the hardware store owner for a 3/8 inch drill that has been languishing for days on the Used & Marked Down pile of weird double-headed screwdrivers, half-dried tubes of caulk, short length extension cords, plastic-packaged do-it-yourself gizmos with no apparent usefulness or value.

In the past six months since he began dialysis he's bored two additional holes an inch apart up the length of the belt beyond the manufactured buckle catches.

His nephrologist is some kind of comedian, a stand-up comic in the clinic. "A dialysis patient's diet regimen," the doctor chuckles—as if he thinks everyone within earshot is in on the common joke—"is like eating cardboard. No more milkshakes, French fries, chimichangas. And that evening cocktail, *nada*. El Boozo is out."

But no one in the adjacent chairs is laughing. They've forgotten how. The dull daily boredom orchestrated by the whirling hum of the machines, the explosive coughing, the hacking of those near death's door, the confined restlessness of those not that far from it, the pointless attempt by everyone undergoing this treatment on any given day within the antiseptic pall of

Just One More Thing (To Go Wrong)

the clinic to push out of mind the thought that in two days you'll be back again for the same tedious four hour link-up—this is what Hub sees, imagines, avoids may times. He cuts short the session today against the liability-laced, paranoid admonishments of the white-clad, masked technicians. Tells them to pull the goddamn tubes out, weigh me, I'm gone. It's my kidneys, not yours.

Mt. Cedar Golden Years served originally as a hospice, then was repurposed for fifty years as the county insane asylum. From a distance, its long, windowed wings jut from a clump of one hundred year old cedars that cap the hill it straddles like a vine covered monastery. The whitewashed brick facade is like a bleached sheet against the stark green grove. To Hub, the ironic history of the place is a circular joke: a haven where one could either die with peace and dignity, or go bonkers, and then shell out for a lottery ticket guaranteeing one last chance in God's Waiting Room.

Hub avoids the main entrance, the disparaged, lowered glances from the nurses and aides on the

Alzheimer's wing. Looks he gets everywhere he goes in New Bastion. He goes in through a rear door where at night they wheel out the recently dead.

Today the bathroom door of his mother's room is closed. He hears the shower running, the muted voice of an aide administering bath time to Mo. Small talk from which there is no answer from the bather.

Hub is dozing in Mo's recliner when the aide leads her out of the bath. Mo clutches the walker like a life support system; she has not been able to walk unaided since the accident. She's still a tall woman who has avoided the shrinkage process that dries up most people her age. The aide has fluffed Mo's close-cropped hair with a dryer, making it resemble a smoked, shredded cigarette filter.

She squints at her son, bobs her head forward, and Hub imagines the gears inside that head meshing against cogs of confusion and, then, recognition: a smile. But she says not a word. Can't, now, another casualty of the hemorrhage.

Just One More Thing (To Go Wrong)

Hub supplies both sides of the conversation today and for the two or three hours a day he sits with her in this small room, enveloped by walls and shelves scattered with the scant memorabilia of a life no longer remembered. Stuff that Ev had evidently rescued from the old house and sent along as a parting gift.

A silver frame at bedside encloses the formal black-and-white wedding portrait of a young couple, the groom a foot shorter than the bride, a plain-faced teenager whose hand-me-down gown is spread out across the floor in front of her like a Chinese fan.

These two kids posed for the camera in the spring of 1954. Whenever Hub asks her who that couple is, Mo jerks back a breath, traces a fingernail over the glass, narrows her eyes as if looking through and beyond the photo, her son, the room. Shrugs as if the *who* doesn't matter—impossible now to conjure. And the *where* no longer exists. And the *what* is of no more concern.

This is how Hub imagines it. This is how he projects what gears are meshing in his mother's damaged brain—if indeed they turn at all. Today he is here to read Everett's letter to her, wonders if he is reciting it only to the walls and to the girl in that long-ago photograph. Wonders if she'll understand any of it. Wonders if the plan he has formulated will also be understood as the only necessity afforded the both of them now that Everett has reneged on the deal and trashed responsibilities he never should have been given in the first place.

2.

It wasn't as easy as Hub had thought to cash out the sunny day fund Everett had deposited with the nursing home. At first, Hub lied to the administrator, said he wanted to buy his mother a new wheelchair to replace the home's supplied one, a raspy sounding older model with one rear wheel that made the thing cant to starboard, which Mo used more and more as her legs gave out.

The administrator, a tight-collared, thin-lipped matron who introduced herself simply as Watling, sneered at Hub during the entire conversation while her narrow eyes scanned this rumpled figure seated opposite her.

She asked if Hub had spoken to his brother lately.

"Because we haven't. He called several weeks ago, but he didn't leave a call-back number." Watling's gaze settled on the flakes of mud Hub had tracked over her office carpet. "And apparently you don't even have a telephone." The woman didn't bother concealing her spite. It was a reaction Hub had come to accept from others, everyone who seemed to act as if they were superior to him—another addendum to his feckless way of life.

"Why do you need to reach Everett?"

"Because he's nearly two months behind on payments. We legally can't put your mother out on the street, but—"

Hub lurched forward. "What are you talking about? You wouldn't actually—"

"We've started legal proceedings," she said, raising her chin as the sneer intensified. "All we have is a Tallahassee address, and our communications bounce back from there. So...as to the one thousand—no. I cannot release it. And you may have to look into an alternative situation for your mother."

Hub had planned to use the money to finance a trip south, familiar back roads— and the dwindling, hard-to-find old-fashioned auto courts he had favored on his travels the few, miraculous times his wallet was flush—all the way, avoiding wherever possible the deadly, crowded, insane interstates.

So now Hub was left with the few hundred dollars he still had crammed into his back pocket. Old Watling's revelation about Everett gave Hub all the more reason to go ahead with his plan. He was now thinking of it as the alternative she had mentioned.

That afternoon Hub scribbled out a note on a 32 cent postcard and mailed it to Everett's Killearn Point Trail address.

Just One More Thing (To Go Wrong)

Ev: Am driving down to see what is going on. I'm bringing Mo with me. You need to explain to us both why you want to put your own mother in the poorhouse. She has lost the ability to speak because of the accident and her memory isn't the best, but I hope she can fully comprehend day-to-day things. I figure we will be there in about 3-4 days from now. —Hub

Hub figured that by the time Ev read it they'd already be on their way: him, Mo—and EmmyLou, fussing and whining in a cramped carrier wedged between a suitcase and his travel-worn knapsack in the narrow space behind the pickup's bench seat. With the ratty nursing home's wheelchair and Mo's walker bungi-corded into the truck bed.

In his haste to get going, Hub had forgotten all about the administrator's remark about letters to Florida bouncing back unopened.

Hub had a couple weeks left on his own prescription meds, and while still at the nursing home that day, he explained to the head nurse that he was taking Mo home for the weekend, and got a three day supply of the rainbow assortment of tabs and capsules she was on. Got a list of the pharmaceutical names of those pills, too. He figured once at Everett's after they knew how long they might stay (permanent, if Hub's plan worked out) he could phone his nephrologist and Mo's resident doc and obtain the necessary refills.

There wasn't a passing thought about continuing dialysis in Florida; he was done with that torment, didn't believe he even needed the treatment in the first place. If anything, he'd get his Medicare to pony up for a second opinion—and most likely ignore that.

Hub had no itinerary for this voyage. Any plan would have been foreign to him. Just the arcing needle of a virtual compass pointing southward is all he needed. If it were possible for Mo to understand that she was going to his trailer for the weekend, by the time they crossed the Ohio River and were meandering through rolling bluegrass hills, past endless ditto rows of white fenced pastures and paddocks—she may have realized (somewhere between her fractured synapses) that, now, there would be no return to Mt. Cedar.

Just One More Thing (To Go Wrong)

Hub studied her as the miles clicked off the odometer, hoping for that twitch of lightning recognition. But Mo, fixated on the undulating scenery, sat like a stone, with no sign of thought or comprehension in her eyes. By Owenton, EmmyLou, too, had resigned herself to what was apparently a new existence: this jouncing, sputtering rush of delirious movement was the way it would always be now; the trailer, the soybean field shielding hidey-holes of baby rabbits and heat-stunned insects—a familiar world of absolute freedom—a past life the cat would soon forget.

Hub carried on a one-way conversation as they drove south, joking about the oddly named villages they past through— Wongo Flats, Gum Sulphur, Dog Walk. Once they got into the Tennessee foothills they'd stopped at a scenic overlook high above the Cumberland Plateau. The little wooden sign read "Hardtack Knob". "Check it out, Mom. They spelled it wrong. But maybe we have relations hereabouts, you think?" But if she was thinking, there was no indication. It was as if for the entire day she saw only the windshield in front of her and nothing beyond.

In the caverns region north of Chattanooga, Hub pulled into the lump-graveled parking lot of Elmo's Tourist Court. The weathered sign at roadside, transformer nearly shot, sputtered a spastic NO P TS ALLOWED, the neon E dangling from its socket. The VACANCY portion was history. It was an hour before darkness, and fog would bleed into the little hollow where the court hid like a ticket to the past.

Hub remembered the place, a row of half a dozen log-framed cabins with rusted roofs and gauzy, narrow windows, from years before when he stood sweating in line at a nearby lumber mill waiting for hours to apply for temp grunt work at slave wages. Work that lasted just two backbreaking weeks. He had rented out a cabin next door to one where a savage and coked-out motorcycle gang who had also signed on for work were busted for cooking meth on a hot plate after their cabin roared into flames one night, causing an evacuation of the entire court, and ending Hub's brief employment. It had no longer seemed like an inviting place to rest.

The cindered rubble of the cabin was still there in a patch of weeds, but Elmo had sold out to a boil-

165

faced Pakistani who resembled a mutant E.T., and who nodded affably behind his glass enclosure when Hub signed in. It was twenty bucks a night. The Pakistani explained that hot plates had been replaced by a microwave in each cabin. He nodded again, toward the burn-out, as if this were an obvious explanation for the upgrade.

Mo had dozed throughout the afternoon's ride and was so stoved-up Hub had to carry her into the cabin and lay her on the rickety bed. She was so still, unprotesting, that Hub wondered if being wheeled out of the nursing home, the gas stops, the clamoring trucks that shot around the sluggish pickup—if any of this even registered with her. Hub had bought a frozen pizza from a convenience store in the last civilized place they had passed through. He brought it into the cabin, sliced it in half, microwaved it as dinner, thumbed quarters into the pop machine outside E.T.'s office for a couple lukewarm root beers. The Pakistani nodded behind his barrier like a bobble-head doll, watched Hub's every move. Maybe tomorrow, if Mo's legs unkinked, Hub thought he would try walking her into a diner somewhere for a decent meal.

Figuring E.T. was serious about NO P TS ALLOWED, Hub waited until after dark to smuggle EmmyLou in from the pickup, along with the bag of her favorite kibbles. The towel carpeting the cat's carrier was soaked and EmmyLou was snarling, clearly wanted out of the deal, clawed at Hub's t-shirt as he bundled the entire mess stealthily into the cabin. Hub went to rinse out the towel and shirt in the bathroom. Maybe take a hot shower. But the water exploding from the faucet was so thick with iron it pooled in the rusted tub like syrup.

That night, after Hub counted out the medications for himself and Mo, he tried to get as comfortable as possible on the floor in his urine-soaked shirt, while Mo drifted off into a dreamless sleep on the bed and EmmyLou cowered beneath it. Hub could smell the charcoal mold, held low to the ground by the evening fog, wafting in from the burned-out cabin. And across the lot, E.T. apparently intended to keep his television set cranked up full blast until dawn. It was the brand of discomfort Hub had long ago accepted as life on his personal planet.

Just One More Thing (To Go Wrong)

Late next afternoon they're in southern Georgia, having given wide drift around the megalopolis warrens surrounding Atlanta and Macon. Taking Mo into a greasy spoon midday was a chore, nearly beyond endurance for both, hoisting the wheelchair out of the truck bed, wrestling a hobbled, confused and by now angry old woman out of the pickup and depositing her into the chair, her legs stiffened and nearly useless with cramps. It was the first time she became vocal, spewing deformed, garbled words he'd never heard her spit out before.

Hub was exhausted by it—the drive, the mounting guilt pressing between his temples that he was doing a really stupid thing here. The bloom was coming off this combined mission of hauling an invalid on a backwater road trip, force-feeding a nearly comatose cat (that had now crawled into an armadillo-like ball in a corner of its carrier), wondering where they would spend the next night, how long was it really going to take at this rate to get to Everett's. Hub was by now two treatments off his dialysis schedule, wondering what poisons were congealing within his kidneys and why his piss the last time was the color of strong tea.

And why he was stopping every hour to spray it painfully into roadside ditches.

For years he had exiled himself, it seemed, so totally over the map, yet these Georgia back roads and swampwater towns—Lollie, Snipersville, Willacoochee— were unfamiliar; he'd never been in this area before. Hub rarely carried roadmaps. Knew he could not get lost. Even in the middle of a moonless night, stars wiped away by an overcast sky, his mental compass—the squirrel spinning like a gyroscope inside his brain— pointed north, south, east, west; whichever way he chose to go.

By nightfall Hub had cut due west of Valdosta and was pressing for the Florida state line. All that afternoon the humidity had soaked into their clothes. Dust, dirt, diesel fumes of semi's he got trapped behind accumulated like microbes inside the pickup cab. Emmylou had saturated the carrier again and the stench of cat urine was like acid in the air. At the last stop Mo had refused to eat and once back in the pickup she had hardened into a rigid trance, her only movement a syncopated foot-stomping against the firewall. Hub

169

Just One More Thing (To Go Wrong)

noticed that Mo's blouse sucked against her body over a layer of sweat, and the steering wheel—which he had been welded to now for nearly twelve hours—felt like a greased yoke in his fists. Hub realized that by continuing another mile he would risk killing them all.

Rather than look for another auto court hidden in the pines in the middle of nowhere, Hub turned off onto a main road and drove until he found the courtyard entrance of a Hampton Inn, one hundred dollars a night. Here was a hot shower, clean sheets, air-conditioning—even a washer/dryer area in a lower hallway. Everything Hub could never afford and always avoided in his travels. But now he felt this respite was owed not only to his own selfishness, but especially to Mo (and even the cat), even if it most likely made little difference, outwardly, to his mother. The inward part, Hub could only guess at. He wanted to project into her barricaded mind at least an ounce of understanding of his motives—motives he was losing his grasp on if, indeed, he ever held on to them at all. Much like gripping the edge of a slippery windowsill, Hub imagined, he on the outside hanging ten stories above the hard ground, waiting for a boot heel to grind against his bloodless fingertips and launch him into freefall.

That night Hub was too exhausted to do much more than cart Mo and EmmyLou into the room and fall into a numb, fitful sleep interrupted only once by a burningly painful piss run. They had until 10 A.M. to check out, so Hub was up by 7:30 to take advantage of the laundry facilities.

When Hub returned, with the dried clothes and underwear and the cat's towel folded neatly into one of the motel's pillow cases, the door to the room was wide open. Mo had somehow managed to sit upright on one of the double beds, and the gate to the cat carrier was canted open, hanging off its hinge.

Hub went to his mother who sat stiffly on the edge of the mattress, rocking back and forth like an autistic, eyes wide, staring at nothing across the room. A rivulet of tears coursed through the spider web wrinkles of her cheeks.

"Mom—what's going on? What's the matter?"

Just One More Thing (To Go Wrong)

Mo's response was guttural, meaningless. Hub tried to help her lay back down, but her legs were frozen into a stinted sitting position; she could do nothing but roll onto her side in a fetal ball. Hub realized it had been more than a day and a night since he'd scooped the meds into her mouth—or, for that matter, taken his own—and he tore into his knapsack for the vials. There was only a paperback he wasn't going to read, a pocketknife, a bag of crumbled chips. He plunged though his pants pockets. Nothing. The meds weren't in the truck—he knew that—because he'd brought everything up to the motel room. Like a raw nerve, it hit him that he must have left the damn things in the filthy bathroom of that shabby auto court the evening before, as tired as he was and hoping for some shut-eye after Emmylou's piss brigade.

And, Jesus—EmmyLou! He dropped to his knees and spun the carrier around, knocking the gate off its hinge. That raw nerve was suddenly like a thousand needles jammed into the back of his neck. He tore the covers off the beds, crawled underneath, swiped his arms in a frenzy, stumbled to his feet and raced into the bathroom, mouth dry, vision spinning, and staggered out to see again the motel door open wide and facing out over the parking lot, and beyond that, the morning traffic heedlessly whizzing by on the roadway. He staggered over to the wash basin and flailed his arms over the ledge, raked off the ridiculous little wrapped bars of complimentary soap and the tiny, useless vial of shampoo, batted the cheap coffee maker, the creamer packets, paper cups wrapped in their sterile pouches across the room and pounded the cheap Formica counter as he dry-heaved into the sink.

There were two Cuban women at the door, the cleaning crew, who couldn't understand a word of the wailing Hub was churning out. They backed off as Hub bolted from the motel room and skirted frantically around the cars in the parking lot, calling for EmmyLou, whistling for the cat as he had done to beckon her out of the soybean field to come inside and figure 8 around his ankles, nudge at him with her wet little nose, get the motor going.

But then he realized that Mo was still on the edge of the bed, was horrified that he had left her unattended and that she might lean forward, fall, hit her

173

Just One More Thing (To Go Wrong)

head, crack open another hemorrhage. He looked back and saw the cleaning women still at the door, waving their broom handles, babbling in rapid-fire Spanish, either unsure whether to enter, or telling him that he and this old woman must leave, time was up. When he returned to the room, calmer now, resigned, he couldn't read the look in Mo's wide, staring eyes, as if there were more going on inside her gnarled brain than the outward blankness belied. He read fear, imagined shame—and realized that Mo must have felt trapped on this voyage, entombed inside her skin; and that by releasing the cat from its bondage she was trying to release herself. Or maybe it was less melodramatic than that; probably the odor of cat piss and the constant whining was what made her kick open the carrier gate allowing Emmylou to disappear forever.

As the cleaning women watched, Hub packed his mother, the wheelchair, the still unopened suitcase and his knapsack into the pickup. He spun out of the lot, headed for Tallahassee, ignoring his stiffened joints, the frozen state of his mother, and at every turn in the road he tried to forget about the cat now gone from his life. Yet he'd kept the carrier, jammed it behind the seat and would use its presence to remind and torture himself that just one more thing could always be counted on to go wrong.

3.

With his distrust of maps (and not giving a good goddamn where he was most times), Hub had always allowed his built-in compass and the curious squirrel pummeling inside his head to give him the freedom to wander without a care of becoming lost.

But it was different now. At a carry-out halfway that day to Tallahassee, Mo spit out the hamburger and fries. The chocolate milkshake he spoon fed her dribbled down her chin, soiled her blouse. Hub couldn't keep anything down either. He could only force himself to chew on a Milky Way bar to keep his glucose level from bottoming out. His legs were leaden posts. Vertigo forced him off the road several times where he spattered the ditches with vomited candy. He could no longer rely

Just One More Thing (To Go Wrong)

on asking directions to Ev's Killearn Point Trails address. He had to put an end to this relentless, ruinous trip. At a gas stop north of Tallahassee Hub gave in and bought a street map of the city.

The Killearn Lakes area northeast of Tallahassee fanned out into concentric wagon wheels of magnolia and eucalyptus lined streets, the spokes dead ending into euphoniously named cul-de-sacs and private drives shielding rambling homes at the edge of what seemed to Hub an endless landscape of lake shores and wide docks where the owners' pleasure crafts bobbed in the waters beyond the mansions.

If it hadn't been for street-side mailboxes, Hub might not have found 1204 Killearn Point Trails. Driving a sputtering, rusted out pickup still caked with red Georgia mud, a wheelchair mounted in the bed and two complete out-of-town strangers in the cab, Hub knew they were the center of attention from neighbors when he parked at the curb in front of Ev's house. A middle-aged man pruning the bushes in his yard next door was checking him out. It wasn't until Hub had stepped out of the pickup that he noticed the unmowed lawn and the sign suspended from a white pole in the front yard:

FORECLOSURE / PRICE REDUCED / IMHOFF REAL ESTATE / 850.397.5000

"Help you, buddy?" The man from next door, brandishing his pruning shears, had sidled up as Hub reached the front door of Ev's house, where the Realtor's lock box hung from the door knob.

"Pardon?" answered Hub. The foreclosure sign, the lock box, the seemingly empty house and now this slightly menacing stranger had made him more disoriented than he already was.

"Can I *help* you?" repeated the man, eyebrows arched, over-emphasizing that word as he loomed closer. The comment was familiar, Hub recognized the look, got it from everyone who saw him: as most likely out of place, perhaps threatening. Hub figured the "help" this guy was offering was helping him off the premises and out of the neighborhood.

Just One More Thing (To Go Wrong)

"The guy who lives here," said Hub. "Everett Hardtak? I'm his brother."

It was like this guy couldn't even bother to hide his close-up survey of Hub's threadbare wardrobe, muddy boots, four day beard stubble.

"They don't live here now, bud."

"They? Ev, Holly—"

"He and his wife moved out a couple months ago. Had to." The man nodded at the foreclosure sign. "Sold most of what they owned at an estate auction. Me and my son helped them move—"

"Wait a minute," said Hub. "What do you mean by 'his wife'? Ev's wife?"

"Yeah," said the neighbor. He backed one step off the porch, having given Hub enough of a once-over. "Quiet woman, that one. Hardly ever came out of the house once she became pregnant. Or we assumed she was. Big girl. Hard to tell, really. Young, though—for a man Everett's age." Now the son-of-a-bitch was going to get chatty while Hub, his head swimming and

178

unfocused, was trying to piece together whatever the hell this guy was talking about.

"And she was kind of sickly, too," the man continued. "I'm sorry, but you didn't know her?"

Hub glanced out at the pickup and at Mo, stiff and motionless as a mannequin. He felt faint; his heart pinwheeled. He wondered if he could remain upright while this guy babbled on, telling him how he and his son and a friend had volunteered to help Everett—*and his wife*—pack up what was left of their meager belongings after the auction and move to a house down in town near the university.

"Must've been a come down for them," the neighbor droned. "Kind of a crummy area." There seemed to be no stopping him now that he had warmed to the subject. Hub felt he was either trying to test his claim as Everett Hardtak's brother, or figure him for some loony with a catatonic old woman in a beat up truck scouting to thieve copper wire. Hub wanted to punch the loud-mouthed idiot, tell him it was none of his business who he was, quit confusing him with details

179

Just One More Thing (To Go Wrong)

that made absolutely no sense. Frightening details. Things about his own brother and daughter that didn't add up. Unraveled things that suddenly he didn't— couldn't—piece together: the foreclosure, Ev evidently broke, the franchise washed away...this guy's mistaken take on Holly...and now Hub was facing even more searching, driving, sickness.

"If you got the address where they moved, please just give it to me," Hub pleaded, wanting to shut the guy up, needing to be away from here before he lost control. "That's our mother there in the truck. She's ill and I'm about wiped. We've been on the road since Friday. I need to get her to my brother's home so she can lay down."

"Better than that, buddy. Hold on." The neighbor, suddenly Mr. Compassionate, trotted over into his house and returned a few minutes later with a sheet of note paper.

"I figure written directions would help, since you're not from around here." He handed Hub the slip. "Just follow this street out to Thomasville Road and hang a left. Then follow my route. You'll find it easy enough. Maybe take you less than an hour."

He swiped his tongue across his upper lip, eyed Hub and Mo. "You sure you two are all right?"

Hub turned and wobbled to the truck without another word, his own tongue like a wad of sandpaper, his legs like rubber bands. 4.

Hub followed the neatly lettered instructions (printed in such a simple way that even the loser this guy evidently took Hub for could follow them) through the city and into a section of narrow streets and single story run-down rentals south of Bragg stadium.

Most of the buildings were painted flamingo pink or washed-out green, with overturned tricycles and scattered toys abandoned in the weedy postage-stamp yards. The garbage trucks must have just come through; dented trash cans had been upturned, a few missed in the collection, remnants of the week's kitchen scraps scattered out into the street.

Just One More Thing (To Go Wrong)

Mo remained static, hypnotized by the air in front of her. Hub had pulled over several times on the drive down from Killearn Lakes just to check the rise and fall of her chest plastered against the sweat and chocolate stained blouse. He could not shake off the trembling that rippled through his legs and back as if he'd either plugged himself into a live electric socket or had been plunged into the icy depths of a sink hole.

Here finally was Ev's house. Someone was peering through the bent slats of a Venetian blind.

Faded lime-green stucco was chipped and falling away from the concrete block structure that fronted on an upheaved, cracked walkway skirting the curbless street. The squat, untended lawn hosted a pile of aluminum beer cans that reflected the glare of a hot noon sun. The entire image was repeated to Hub up and down the street as if these houses, the trash, the unkempt lawns were part of an inward reflecting house of mirrors.

Hub was near nausea as he approached the front door where his brother stood with a speechless look of wonder, surprise, perhaps (Hub thought), a gray wash of guilt—as behind Everett, half hidden in the blue shadows within the house, wavered Holly, who also looked to have not the faintest clue.

"You didn't get my postcard, did you Ev?" Hub thought to pull the screened door open when his brother did not move. But he hesitated and said, "It wasn't forwarded. My guess you didn't even bother to leave a forwarding address. Or didn't want to."

Everett was transfixed like a granite statue of apathy but stepped aside just enough to reveal Hub's daughter ballooned out in the glory of her third trimester, tented by a bleached-out smock that draped over her filthy bare feet. Neither Ev nor Holly offered a word.

Hub had not wanted to appear angry or even stunned himself when he showed up on this doorstep. He had fantasized and rehearsed and fictionalized this reception every hour night and day, all the way down from New Bastion, and so no longer was sure of what he believed, or doubted, or denied now that he was here in front of these two, his closest remaining kin besides the one still waiting and immobile in the cab of his pickup who might be entertaining thoughts—if she had any at all at this stage—that might be equally as jumbled or incoherent as his own and those (he had to figure from looking at them now, close-up, behind the hole-patched screen) of his brother and pregnant daughter standing like zombies a nose length away in front of him at the door.

"That's our mother out there, Ev." Hub turned and started to walk back to the pickup, and behind his back said, "You need to help me bring her inside."

* * *

Photo: David Schrieber

W. Jack Savage

california, usa

wjacksavage.com

W. Jack Savage is a retired broadcaster and artist who now writes and draws full time. He is the author of five books: three novels and two short story collections.

Jack and his wife Kathy live in Monrovia, CA.

186

Veterans at the Post Office

Carl felt stiffer than usual that Thursday morning but there was nothing wrong with his sense of wonder. As he carefully negotiated the two steps down into the main lobby of the post office and took his place fourteen customers back in line, he quickly processed that while he couldn't exactly remember, he was pretty sure there were no lines at the post office in the old days: certainly not on a Thursday morning in May.

In recent years, Carl had aged noticeably but even so, still felt somewhat self-conscious about his thinning hair. With a good shampoo and a little work with the hair dryer you really couldn't tell but that morning he'd finished up a story and was in a hurry to get it mailed and so he put on a baseball cap instead. He held onto his four Manila envelopes with corresponding envelopes folded in half and partially sticking out. There were four places for postal workers to assist customers

187

but only two were ever manned. He knew if he got the little Asian girl at the counter everything would be fine. She knew what he wanted: four stamps to mail each package and then exactly the same postage to put on the inside envelopes to achieve 'Self Addressed Stamped Envelope' status for their return. Then, after putting them all on and sealing each with the return envelopes inside, the biggest part of his day would be over.

"Excuse me?" a young woman in her twenties said behind him.

He turned and looked and smiled, now sure it was he that she was addressing. She was a sort plain looking girl with a very nice posture, he thought.

"Yes?"

"Were you with the 1st Cav?"

Carl seemed confused as to how this young woman or even why she should care if an old guy like him was in the 1st Cavalry Division?"

188

"Why yes," he said with a nod and a smile. Then it hit him. He was wearing the 1st Cav hat his niece had bought for him somewhere.

"Sorry," he said. "I didn't realize I had a hat on. I wondered how you knew."

"I was in the 1st Cav too," she said, as they both shuffled up another spot in the line.

"I see," he said. "Uh, and where did you serve?"

"Well, I would have served in Iraq," she said, "but a week before my unit left Germany I was in a car accident. They sent me home after that."

That's ah," he began, "I mean I'm sorry about your accident but it's kind of strange. The same sort of thing happened to me; although, I was already in Vietnam when it happened. It ended my time in country and in the service. Just a stupid accident."   Carl shook his head and said, "I wonder, did you kind of feel cheated that you didn't get a chance to go over?"

Veterans at the Post Office

She smiled and said, "At first I did, yeah. But in the end I guess I was lucky. Several members of my company were killed the first week"

"I suppose you know we lost our colors in Korea and they started the division back up for Vietnam. I was with the 1st of the 8th."

She nodded.

"I guess, I got cheated out of seeing action too: not unlike you. I saw some before, before the accident."

They shuffled up a few more places and she said "What happened?' she asked. "If you don't mind my asking?"

"We were walking down the road that led to the helicopters to take us out to the field. It had rained the night before and it was real muddy so we were kind of walking close to the edge where it was dryer. There were some guys digging out the ditch alongside the road. I guess one of them swung his pick back and hit my head. I woke up in Japan and they said my skull was fractured and that I was going home."

They both smiled at each other and nodded.

"At first I felt like, if I was gonna get hurt that bad, it should have been in combat, ya know? But so many guys got killed, some later that day, that I guess I was lucky."

Now only four people were ahead of them.

"Women didn't serve in those days did they?" she said.

"Sure they did, mostly nurses but a lot of other stuff. They were WAC's, you know. I used to see them training at Fort Gordon, Georgia where I took my AIT. I don't know how you do it today, living in the same barracks. I just can't imagine it."

She nodded and said, "It's different."

"It's just guys, ya know? Some guys turn into complete idiots around women, especially at that age."

"It goes both ways, actually," she said. "It's tough sometimes."

Veterans at the Post Office

Now with only one customer ahead of them, Carl extended his hand and said. "Carl Gundrum."

"Jackie Kittles," she said shaking his hand.

"Can I help the next customer?" said the little Asian woman postal worker.

After getting all his postage and affixing it and sealing it all up for mailing, Carl paid with his credit card and headed off. When he got outside he saw Jackie Kittles.

"Hi," he said again.

"Can I ask you a question, Mr. Gundrum?" she said.

"Sure you can but call me Carl, Jackie."

"It seems like you were born through the Korean War and served in Vietnam. There've been several wars since then. Has being a veteran changed how you look at wars in general?"

Carl nodded and said, "Yes. Because when you served, when you joined and went through training and were willing to fight, whether you fought or not it kind of gives you an elitist feeling. I mean, I can find fault with all those wars, any of those wars. But because I was a volunteer for one of them, it's like my point of view means more than people who never served. I know that's awful but that's how I feel sometimes. I shouldn't because in fact, I saw some action but not that much and certainly not enough to give me nightmares or anything. I was sent home after being injured in an accident like you. It makes me feel bad to admit it but that's the way I feel sometimes. You're young. What's your experience so far?"

"Mine's a little different," she said. "You see I lost my left leg below the knee in the accident. I'm a veteran, a disabled veteran but without explaining everything people don't get the whole picture. They naturally assume I lost my leg in combat and it's like you said, since I volunteered for that combat, I almost feel entitled to let them think that. But being a woman, people don't see you as a veteran: they don't imagine that. It doesn't matter to guys at all. They just see you as having part of one leg missing. How it happened doesn't seem to matter to them. Most of them would rather have a girl with two legs. That's just the way it is."

Carl nodded gravely and said, "I can see that. But it's kind of funny when you think about us being veterans. I'd never buy a hat like this for myself and rarely wear a hat at all. It's really the only hat I have and yet without it, you'd never think to ask if I was a veteran and I'd not only not think to ask you, because of the era I served in, I'd have never known you had part of your leg missing. At my age, when you asked me if I was in the 1st Cav, I was muttering under my breath about having to wait in lines at the post office. When I was your age there were no lines. I guess what I mean is it's six of one and half a dozen of the other. Things have been lost over my lifetime but a lot of things are better too. Wars never seem to make sense and if they do, it's only at the beginning. But even knowing that we still have them. Let me ask you this: in my day a young woman like you might experience war as say, having a brother who served or maybe even your dad. Then, once you have children it would be worrying that war might touch them when they grow up. Do you think you feel any different as things are now and having served?

"I don't know," she said. "Because you see it goes back farther then that. When you were growing up, on the playground were there as many girls playing games as there are today?"

"No, I guess not, now that you mention it. Girls played with dolls, I guess."

"They still do but what I'm saying is, we were raised to be more, think more and told we could be anything we wanted. From what my mom told me, that's all new. So in a way, I'm a product of that as much or more than having served in the army. Do you have any children?"

"No, I never got married. I was engaged once but that accident left me with seizures and I guess it was just easier finding some guy who didn't have them. After a while I just quit looking for that. It kind of made me bitter when it didn't work out and bitter is worse than having seizures. Later on they came up with treatments you know and the seizures went away. By that time I was kind of set in my ways. So I guess I missed that part about seeing how kids grow up compared to how it was for me."

Moments later it would be over and Jackie and Carl would shake hands and go their separate ways. It had been invigorating for both of them and each would think about their exchange for quite a while. The truth is, outside of families, men in their sixties and young women in their twenties don't have enough in common to meet as strangers and talk for fifteen minutes or so. But people still have wars in common and the people who fight in them tend to view each other more equally than might ordinarily be the case. Carl would think about these things for some weeks and finally, put a version of it down on paper. Not long after, as he stood in line at the post office to send off his story to the submission's editors of several magazines, he began to think of all his recent experiences and sending off his stories as a sort of clearing house for what his life had become. As he did on that particular day, his sense of indignation at waiting in line at the post office seemed nowhere to be found.

massachusetts, usa

Tom Sheehan

massachusetts, usa

Tantra Bensko **CARLY BERG** *Ute Carson* TONY CONCANNON Rudy Ch. Garcia

Margaret Karmaz

Manish Singh Hollis

Tony Concannon RUD

Tom S

Wp

KA

WH

RUI

She

T

HoL

Cars

SHE

BEI

JAf

V

C

G

Sheeh

Wyat

Mar

WH

CAR

Jack

T

I

S

> Tom Sheehan served in 31st Infantry Regiment,
> Korea, 1951-52, and graduated Boston College, 1956.
>
> He has 20 Pushcart nominations, 340 stories on Rope
> and Wire Magazine (and never been on a horse),
> work in Rosebud Magazine (5), The Linnet's Wings
> (6) out of Galway, Ocean Magazine (8), and many
> internet sites/print issues/anthologies including
> Nervous Breakdown, Eskimo Pie, Faith-Hope-Fiction,
> Subtle Tea, Danse Macabre, Deep South Magazine,
> Best of Sand Hill Review, Best of Frontier Tales,
> Wilderness House Literary Review,
> MGVersion2Datura, Dew on the Kudzu, Literary
> Orphans, Eastlit, and Nazar Look, etc. His work has
> been published in Romania, France, Ireland, England,
> Scotland, Italy, Thailand, China, Mexico, Canada, etc.
>
> Tom Sheehan waits for two more mysteries to be
> published in 2013 and some western short story
> collections, seven completed including covers by his
> sons.

RUDY CH. GARCIA *Margaret Karmazin* JAMES D. REED Wl.

eehan Hollis Whitlock **SAMUEL K. WILKES** *Abigail Wyatt*

Carly Berg **Ute Carson** TONY CONCANNON *Rudy Ch. Garcia* **MARGARET**

S. D. REED W. Jack Savage **Tom Sheehan** Bhadauria Manish Singh

BIGAIL WYATT *Tantra Bensko* CARLY BERG **Ute Carson Tony**

Concannon RUDY CH. GARCIA *Margaret Karmazin* **JAMES D. REED** W. Jack Savage

Tom Sheehan **Bhadauria** **Manish Singh** Hollis Whitlock Abigail Wyatt **TANTRA BENSKO**

Carly Berg UTE CARSON Tony Concannon **Rudy Ch. Garcia** MARGARET KARMAZIN *JAMES*

D. REED **W. JACK SAVAGE** *Tom Sheehan* Bhadauria Manish Singh Hollis **Whitlock** Samuel

Lover, not Yet Lover

And so it was, plain and simple, a necessary thing to do, an oath moving in one's self at the beginning of resolve, a slow upward presence, a climbing of spirit, so that he saw it coming as if from a field of mist caught out atop a

199

Lover, not Yet Lover

pasture, the morning young, dew spread and spent under the sun exerting itself always, and with it all he saw the outcome, how it would come down the line swift as a memory in some far place where he was out of this habit range, this wide place he might have called home grounds except it was not solicitous at the time, and that memory, as stark as it might be at the finish of its appearance, would come like that same mist off the grass, at first as conceivable, then as probable, and finally, with a conscious note of thanksgiving, come whole and moving and it would be her in a final presence in the same place, in his heart and not his mind, in his heart and not behind his eyes where he thought he'd see it again and again, in his heart and not in his hands the way he'd recall her at odd moments of the night with a twist and a turn and a sigh, but sleep now a dread enemy, sleep an impossibility, sleep that came of wretched evasion and long mourning, and just as always she'd be visible in a new haven, looking at him, her chin in hand, blue eyes as wide as ever, and sending him that continual message, only to have it waylaid by someone other than either one of them, another body in her place, a new touch, a new taste, a woman of thought, a woman possible, perhaps around the corner, perhaps at the next cup of tea, perhaps a pair of eyes he'd know would be her eyes in the second place of their coming, and he'd roll over and hate himself and cry his poor soul to sleep.

Where it all began and might end had come upon him as surprise comes to any alert soul, her illness an unaccustomed turn, a brevity of concern at first, a slight indication of some small piece not working, the way it happens in ordinary door chimes, the least of importance, for the knock would follow and the entrance conducted and the gaiety loosed once more, or then, more thorny, as in a clock where a spring might be caught unawares or a notch filled with debris or a gear snagged, and time, by the minute, would go its way, or an hour, to the end of the month where some due would get undone, unfinished, lost.

He'd know his loss more than separation, more than death.

She had the last words saved up for a delivery meticulous and persuasive: "Do not stop what you are doing; do not chase after me in any hurry; and in all loyalty and bound by this promise, find someone to talk to, to read to, to release to."

He brought himself back to a new day where it would begin for him, coming that ordinary way, in a soft hour of evening as the sun tipped its hat goodnight at the kitchen window and across the room in a friend's house he could see her acknowledging again one of her last days, in that special way she had of salutation, reminding him how everybody on God's hard earth loved her, the patients whose cries she could hug, the nurse orderlies that she trumpeted to all and sundry, how they had come from devastation and nothing to hope for, unto this place of hope, agreeing with her that all should be pain free and exalted in their dignity, even as all those days dwindled into sobs few heard but her at the door of the room, at the end of the hall, with the last step from the inside of that huge place to the outside, the evening blessing her tired moves, her muscles, her spirit looking for nourishment for the day to follow, for surely repetition was the sin there.

He knew how it would happen.It began for him, across a room in that friend's home where people mixed in merriment and talk of another loss and celebration, the babble and groundswell moving in slight waves keeping all corners alive not with the same words but with the same intents ... the look, the approach, the answer, the assent without a sound, agreement working the fields of the bodies in the large room, in the field of his body, that new pair of eyes saying all the things he might want to hear, putting aside judgments and comparisons, putting aside the cause of the initial attraction, because her eyes were running with the words he could not hear but understood, the way semaphore flags at the lip of an aircraft carrier can spell its position and its acceptance to a pilot winging his way home, out of gas, praying for the lap of safety, the parts all together for maybe the last time in this life.

Later, the stub of afternoon coming spent, the one with the announcing eyes would point out the window to three children of the neighborhood playing in a side lawn of a neat house whose red bricks had taken on a dusky red hue the sun has some days in late summer, whose hedges were trimmed by a barber with comb and scissors, and whose windows must have been dressed by a quaint old lady who had asked for one more turn at decoration to carry her name and her last thought caught up in a pairing of colors.

This mere stranger for the moment, who had come from across the room at the beginning of her place in all of this, with her own loss, stared at the children, a light falling across her face, across the lenses of her eyes in the way those children ought to be seen, in a choice part of the inner eye, a roll call brought to bear with their histories coming on, the schools of their growing years assembled piecemeal in the new fiction as though they were now promised, or had been promised long before these new parents had come on the scene to make their wishes, to say their prayers, to offer their thanksgivings.

Her voice had a mysterious quality in it. "Let's make them ours." She said it with soft passion, with an eye on their clocks, and with solemn promise, as if it had already happened, that mini-adoption, that quick attachment. "Let's watch them whenever we can, as obliged we would be, enjoy their goodness ahead, their coming small sadness, see them leap up and onward, and hold them dear as we ought in the silence of our hearts. That is the most of love I can muster."

The words that followed might have been spoken before, by her of the past.

"Let's be in love again, each of us, with all possibilities for as long as we can." She took his hand and held it close and in another moment he knew she'd move his hand upon the promise.

The nights would say their names and it would be enough to hear the soft syllables.

And so the way it was supposed to happen, it did, love advancing the soul's illumination of inner light, the mass of it coming at once, at first an illusion so beautiful it was previously unimagined, and then, after his wanton sleep was beset and circulated with toss and turn and turmoil, and with a side glance at once mistrusted but leaving a hard dent in his memory, she moved from the covey of her own shadow into the scan of his horizon, and remains in that one spot, that totally owned place by herself, a grace emanating from that

Lover, not Yet Lover

aura unseen as music but the tempo and the unbidden language coming along with it, the rhythm of a woman who moves with ease into the depth of a man where she assimilates, absorbs, animates by a motion so subtle to this day it still overpowers him .

She moved like the appreciation of a mountain morning hovering over a lake, a mist slow in ascension to translate into an unseen level allowing iridescence of innumerable growths to appear in a painting his eyes said existed solely for his vision, at the moment no other person seeing what he was seeing; and in its climbing into a nothing that did exist for his wonder and awe, became the other side of the lake, she in one image he had put away for all time as that one image to salvage him from despair and loss so unequivocal it promised no future to his natural hunger and need; knowing from the inception she was a dream come alive for him, this woman, a mere mist at first, coming alive, a smile wide as horizons, coming alive, a voice saying she was real, coming alive, its tone so meticulous and full of clarity it struck him with lightning delivery, the first word coming alive his name, the very first sound saying she was thinking of him and beset with the energies and want that had littered his days and nights steady as cast-off memories shunted aside but never letting go, the other truths hanging on, past dear life.

His name came softly in the night, in the truth of darkness, on the breath of a woman moving the way only a woman moves, a languorous length of her, a gloried broadness, a hip salutation as much signature as identification, into his mind before all else, into the spirit sitting there alone and waiting for the word, the gesture, the hand sending its touch on a linen full of sound but so silken and smooth it was as if his name came carried there first, the manner of the passage as much invitation as any invitation might be broadcast from soul to soul, the call heard and the reply sent outward, the elegant length of her reduced, brought closer, a loop in its coming, a grasp, a homing brought to bear his all, an ascension of will silent at first but then pounding in his heart, and then to his mind where it evolved as the transfer of love more monumental yet existing in that languorous depth beneath him in a grip only her kind owned.

Lover, not Yet Lover

He said her name, and it rose pious, devout, though of a second nature, an element about in the night like an unseen feather on unseen air but letting off a whisper of sound, a whisper of such promise and continuity it came of soul salvage, of mere dreaming, of harnessed energy, of the ultimate connection of essence and turmoil mixing the grander ingredients where imagination alone is the king, the guidepost, the whip soft as bee flight, as positive, her grasp essential.

Then, in brevity of concern, of conscience, he heard her voice as from the far end of a tunnel, or the top of a mountain so distant it was out of sight, the soft syllables advancing on him the way balm dissolves worry and fright, the way it descends on the ache in a spirit.

It was necessary now, he thought, the time arrived for it to happen, and he moved a ways and looked behind him and saw how far he had come in this loneliness, in this short time, and it was bigger than an ache, and it moved on him as slow as he thought about himself and then her, and there was silence he could not comprehend, which made him think of being a distant star looking back here and saw himself less than he was and knew the difference, knowing nothing of time, only of manner --- how it happened, not why, not where, but knowing the form of it.

It was her.

* * *

The Storekeeper

Before I knew what was going on, at twelve years of age, I saw what was going on... with Putney Grimes, who owned the Pioneer Grocery and General Store near my house, and one of his customers, Maxine Greenery. Truth of the matter was I didn't know what I was actually seeing, or couldn't understand it until much later, but parts of this life were moving around me, memories as well as history being made, records being kept, innocence being expelled one way or another, true innocence. World War II, of course, was trampling on a whole tide of innocence. Glad tidings said General MacArthur was back in the Philippines, but on the other side of that, Glenn Miller was reportedly lost in the North Sea. My mother looked dreamy-eyed at that news, the way she could share some things without talking about them. In my own little way, then with just those dozen years in hand, I knew I was part of it all, part and parcel. Pieces of it enveloped me, or lifted me, or brought me down; experience building its everlasting testimony.

As for Putney and Maxine, a warmth was in our midst, in spite of the shape of the world, even if I could not give it a name. I couldn't name it and I couldn't touch it, but it was there. It all centered in the store, small heart of the universe we knew. Much later I could call myself, in retrospect, the love child because I saw the love blooming between them right there in front of me, day by day, even though it took more than a few years time, and I, of course, in my own growth, felt the changes.

The Storekeeper

The way it was for a while was that Maxine Greenery could be a widow for all we knew, and with two sprouting boys. The hard words came one evening just as supper hit the table and twilight was still holding sway, the shadows soft, day dwindling down to its knees: her husband Harry had been declared missing, lost at sea from a destroyer in the Mediterranean Sea, half a world away, a lifetime away. Shadows joined with shadows, loss atop loss. George Drew, the Fire Chief, brought the word. He was the self-appointed dispenser of the awful tasks in his snappy uniform, black gloves, white hat, pants pressed so that the creases were like sheet metal lines, and all blue, the length of him all blue. When he tucked his white hat under his blue arm, every person on the street knew it was not an inspection of the premises being approached, the slow walk into a front yard, the unhurried climb to the porch, the soft tap on the door. And nothing followed that first announcement of the loss of Harry. No whispers. No rumors. Loss settled on us, heavy as one could imagine.

Harry was one of the good guys around our corner before he left, and Maxine was seen as a regular customer of Putney's. She had been a customer since

Harry put her in that converted barn he had worked on for Ladd Griffin just around the turn from Putney's store, when he went off in the Navy. Harry was a magician with hammer and saw, good old Harry, and had the acute eye for resurrection, bringing old lines of structures into new lines, new plumbs, walls standing the way they were meant to stand, with the good shoulders. In due time, the way promise evolves, as all the neighbors had said almost at once when he went away, that Harry would build his own house when he came back, when his turn came up, but those chances were now gone and slim at best, it appeared.

But the main guy here from my angle, Putney Grimes, owned and was the sole employee of the Pioneer Store in my end of town, near the first Iron Works in America that lay untouched for more than 300 years. When my pals and I had a few spare coins, Putney's store was where we ended up, a post-Depression magnet for kids used to grasping. Many of my friends had found labor to our liking, our stretch to manhood, the war moving at far edges, almost visible, the way we saw the Newsreels at the State Theater on Saturday matinees. And we had small jobs then, paying small change. We had a lot to do with scrap metal drives, paper collections, keeping our lips zipped, pretenses of one sort or another.

Earlier, in a stretch toward manhood, we had carried baskets of manure and sterilized loam into the old mushroom house on Lily Pond. It used to be an ice house before Freddie Rippon converted it to a mushroom house where, if the crop was fairly large and there was no disease, he could make some good money. As kids we shared that whole enterprise, eventually loading trucks going off to the market in Boston, filling our pockets with slim coins while mothers sat at their kitchen tables waiting for donations.

As it was, most of my pals had a handle on such tasks in Saugus, closing in on the mid-century mark, money times better than they had been for a handful of years, and some of the old guys that made it back from Europe and the Pacific were comfortably on leave or medically discharged, enriching all of us with new gestures, new stories, seemed like a whole new language. They brought their pieces of the world back with them, dumping much of it in our laps, the laps of those who had stayed at home, the kid brothers and kid neighbors and those who couldn't make the fit. My brother came back from the wild Pacific, right off an aircraft carrier twice hit by Kamikazes and once by a torpedo, never telling us until he got home, and my cousin Warren came back from Europe after Patton shook his hand in front of a gathering of troops out there on the edge of the Old World. Pretty special for a Saugus kid.

On the other hand, a few of their comrades managed to slip off the trains in Saugus Center near midnight, coming right out of North Station and the Army Base or the Charlestown Navy Yard, like they were total strangers. And I guess some of them were, they had changed so much, had seen so much. All their stories, though, came as gifts, long into our new nights of discovery, a new expression, a new outlook, a new hope even as we realized many of the dark parts were being glossed over. Some did not make the return trip and there was a time when I knew all their names and all their faces, what they had left in the till for me, a kid from this end of town.

The Storekeeper

Putney's Pioneer Store was where much of the talk and information passed from hither and yon to all the houses in our end of Saugus. He carried a whole arsenal of goods besides the usual grocery items; most of the time catering to the ladies with cloth goods, small hats, big bowls, you name it and he'd get it. He specialized in information too. You could tell that Put was eager for all kinds of intelligence, as though he had been selected to be a communication center, keeping people informed, ranking news, passing tidbits that ordinarily didn't plan much hurt for anybody. Some things, I knew, he kept to himself, letting others pass the word, as if he was a sieve screening out the bad parts.

I think it was the melancholy of the war that mostly triggered Putney, changed his expression, changed his manners, and damn near changed his language. The war and its odd pieces daily came down the street and through his door like the wind had kicked it open, like the words of another telegram hitting straight at a heart or two, or a distant shot or shell seeming to come home to the storekeeper in a gulp of morning air, as though aimed at him from the very beginning. All this culminated for him in Maxine and

her current status as "widow." He was the on-looker
who cared even though it was at a polite distance. They
regarded each other in these times with awareness, each
of them at some point of loss, at loneliness or linen.

Then, in days of recovery, when the war was
finally being won, Putney and Maxine were allowed to
be drawn by their needs. As it stood, the future loomed
lonely for both of them. When Maxine was in the store,
she was always visible to Putney, who would put himself
to that advantage no matter what aisle he was working
in or who he was waiting on. He did it casually, not at all
obvious to most other customers, but a perfect
chameleon to my eyes. On odd occasions he'd let me sit
beside the side door and read comic books for free, as
long as I did not crease them too much. It was a
measure of his charity, of the blossoms that ripened in
his heart. From my spot at the side door I had a view
down the front counter and down the back aisle. The
first time Maxine stretched to put something back on a
higher shelf, a packet or container she had dislodged
from its place, I caught a half smile on Putney's face,
though at the moment he was waiting on the
neighborhood witch, Ethel Nourseling, my old teacher

The Storekeeper

with the strap or the harsh ruler for a wayward tongue. Maxine always wore dresses that seemed to have been slipped onto her slim frame, silky and soft and smooth the way they flowed with her curves and graces and all the goodly package; that package contained blond hair soft as a summer cone, wide eyes that surprise found a good home in, lips a favored pink blossom had touched just about every time out, and a warmth, a warmth that was never spectacular, not for those of us who looked closely, but always countable, easily marked and noted, as though a small party had started someplace and she was invited.

Putney, a bachelor all the way to forty, was not a handsome dog, as one wag said, but he was neat. You might know it... grocers tend to be neat, sort of going along with the territory... everything in its place to catch they eye, the silent art of advertisement, the handless reach. Things that look good might taste good, or feel good. To boot, certain facets of Put's behavior ought to be mentioned for the best picture of him. For absolute sure, he knew the store the way a woman knows her kitchen, shelf and larder, cabinet and cupboard, the bins and barrels at the end of the main aisle like greengrocer totems... what's stacked where, or put behind, what's left in easy reach and another tucked away under the counter for special days, or consigned for the next special sale or holiday. His clock, or his calendar, was pretty near perfect for his customers, for our neighborhood. Now and then we'd see it working, the close lookers among us, like him spotting old Della Crandall coming down the street and dipping below the counter to lay out what had been hidden for more than a week, a new bolt of cloth or an infernally new utensil the adventurous lady would grab in a minute. They'd been ordered for her and salted away for the most appropriate visit, as if old Put had a hand directly on her pulse, on her current interests.

In addition, he always wore an apron that was adorned with the day's work, wore it like a good soldier wears his chevron, as one might say. He was proud of his work, his store, and he was potentially if not actually prosperous. As a stock boy he had worked there for the previous owner, went away for ten years, came back and bought the place, as if he had planned it right from the very start. His hello each morning was broad, meaningful, countable, him having risen early to greet

The Storekeeper

the day, to be there before the baker and the milkman and the newsboy. Early energy became him, the quick movements, the lack of indecision, jump starts on a new day. One man operations have to be fed that way.

His razor thin mustache was little more than a hairline's width, and moved each time he spoke, smiled or expressed want or dislike. I never really knew what color his eyes were; I guess I never really looked, though they did come off as some kind of greenish bit, sort of changeable under other expressions or enlightenment. Narrow in the waist from a lifetime of shelf stocking and lifting, and a sane and steady diet one could imagine, he moved about athletically, as if he were in a game. Neat and athletic our grocer. On top of the small ladder he could stock the top shelves with good speed, never losing balance, reaching just far enough when he had to. The neatness advanced in order to the store's ambience, the certainty of odors that abounded on certain days, on every day of some sort or other. There came coffee grinding and candy smothering my mouth and nose the minute I entered the door. It had been that way for a couple of years, the grateful larder of the corner store, pungent and ripe and so full of goodness I could feel the blossoms of it coming into the branches of me. There was the fresh vitality of new bread, fresh baked and threatening the back of my throat, saying I could grab some and run, or scrounge for a half loaf, and worry about the butter later on. And jumped up the freshness of lettuce and husky tomatoes and apple stuff so rich it could make your knees bend. Lastly, just as threatening, came the special meat days, when pork came on the run or cow's liver or lamb kidneys advancing a whole new odor the kitchen got ripe with. Some days it could have been the edge of the slaughterhouse dumped on us, or the block outside Kmita's chicken house where the ax swung in morning sunlight and I could see a hen's last roost as darkness came close to it. I finally figured a whole lot of it out, all on my own... I had always been hungry, the Depression Kid always with an angle toward food.

Once, just as the door opened and a whistle of wind came about, or an airy breath because it was spring, Putney came to attention. I caught the scent too, the fragrance, not of the day or the May smells that came along in with it, like new leaves and new blooms and the old earth winding itself up again, but another and newer one, especially for me... and old Put, hardly paying attention the minute before, spun on his heels and Maxine was there, slim as ever, in her light blue dress sitting on her like a blossom, inhabiting the doorway. There was first the alert of fragrance, then the heart of fragrance, and a rocking in our souls, in deeply where it must count, where redolence, known, gathers all kinds of reactions. It was a sharing, that frequency coming on air, a quite special broadcast of a special bouquet. It fully carried Maxine on those private sheets of air.

And old Putney was at heads up. And Maxine glowed her usual warmth, as if she belonged in that place more than any place else, in the midst of all the sensual goodness. To my eye he and Maxine each had a fair amount of grace. I think, even from my angle, I put them together before they were together, though I'd never be sure of the timing.

Some of it meant, at least for me, that it was okay for them to look upon each other, that it was okay to look good, look neat, look to one's best advantage, if merely for the looking. It was permission from two lonely people not saying a word about such acceptance. Every time a teacher said, "Neatness counts," I was alert to Putney and Maxine, if but the extension of their images working the back of my head like a piece of a black and white film. Now and then, of course, in my mind's eye, going through my own exploding new dimensions, I was alert to her preparations, as to how she primped and primed herself, where she sent the kids while she did so, at least not alerting them that their mother was being a bit selfish, reaching out in a most harmless way but behind a closed door, locked away with herself and whoever might be tempting her company.

Putney was harmless from any standpoint, but he had keen eyes. I was always sure that she knew about his eyes. And I knew how her dress slipped easily onto her frame, thought of how she might have shrugged but a single shoulder to let it fall gracefully in place, and fully assumed that Putney had the same picture, the soft sounds of elegance and mystery coming together in the same motion, the same slow blur of beauty that might be slipping into place from a simple shrug.

The Storekeeper

When Doug Matlick's body was shipped home from a Marine plane crash in North Carolina and lowered into the Veteran's Section of our cemetery, I was there with my father who had been in the Marines. It was his own salute to Doug. Doug was Harry's best friend. Putney saluted too, the only time I ever saw him in a suit, plain and gray and new looking, and never once looking at Maxine the way he did in the store, for Maxine was there, being an old friend of Doug's. Before I knew it, we were there again, for another of Harry's friends who had come home for good, almost able to touch his old pal and teammate Doug, for they were now part of a new huddle in a corner of the cemetery, close as they ever were. For sure, teammates again.

I knew every face at both services and the burials and could mark each of them in their places around town, and felt all the sadness you could expect a body to hold. I didn't cry, though, did not a shed tear, but when I looked at Putney I saw he was shaken past his roots. It was as if everything all the others had felt closed in around him, and around Maxine who only once turned and looked at him with the most serious look I had seen in a long time. It was as if she had spoken, but with silence.

I watched them for two years as the slim war victories became big victories, and more of them came rousing across the face of the globe. The two of them eventually seemed to grow toward each other without really knowing how close they were.

Wiley Okens said at The Vets one night that "them two ought to find how to scratch each other's backs 'stead of sparrin' around like pretending." Many folks in town knew that Maxine was finding a bit of release in Putney from what was hounding her, the squeezed pillow, the silent nights. Putney allowed her more than a sense of hope, but all of it at a distance no matter how close they got on days she came to the store to pick up a few things for the house. Even when there were days it came off as mere exercise to walk to the store and go away empty-handed, she did not leave with an empty heart. Yet, at forty years of age, distilled in his manners and outlook, damn near cemented in place if not character, Putney had that one old-time speed. Of course, Maxine's two boys would now and then enter

The Storekeeper

into the slow-moving stand-off of sorts, tipping the scales in pro and con arguments the way kids do more than people realize. Malcolm Burdus the undertaker offered, "One mouth advanced to four mouths is some kind of algebra no matter what math says."

Putney's down to earth and thoughtful approach was appreciated by those who voiced opinions on romance, illicit or otherwise. "He don't rush that girl out of her boots none at all," Malcolm told Wiley one night and later on said, "If he don't hurry up, I'm going to beat him to it." All of them somehow knowing that Putney had ceased a regular Saturday night removal from town that was seen as a concession to Maxine and the space that had grown in his heart.

"Hell," Wiley replied, "he's got all the time in the world, Malcolm, and you got all the room in the earth. But I'm suspecting that ole Put has just that one speed and we ain't seen it yet." So the talk moved on about them, and the store leaped upon good days for Putney when Maxine came in through that front door like spring was sliding around behind her playing games.

All the time, no matter how we read it, the unknown sat on the face of each of them, the uncertainty, the Fates that move all around us like the tides on a beach, touching, drawing back, nipping and tapping, neap and run, like the manner of unvoiced threats and promises.

As it turned out, things happened at night to old Putney. It was always at night or the approach of night as it gathered down the street or from across town and he could feel a descent coming down around him.

One evening, almost to closing time on one of his late night closings, a shower and a visit to the library ahead of him, two young fellows robbed bachelor Putney of what was in the till. The eleven dollars, all singles, were hardly worth their efforts, as he had hidden under darkness the balance of the day's take inside a pair of rubber boots hanging on the wall behind the counter, safe enough for the bank in the morning. But one of the young fellows snatched a candy bar as he and his companion were leaving with their eleven dollar gain. It was a Sky Bar. All Putney could think of was somehow getting a box of candy to Maxine, then he realized he hadn't been shot for eleven dollars. He told that to the police chief, in so many words.

Then, on another night in our local history, without notice or fanfare, from what unknown terrors he had been caught up in, and much older, Harry came home, came into the store late, as if riding the darkness itself, the ghost of all ghosts, despite the edge of his voice yet still haggard and not at all like his old self. He hailed Putney from the door. "Hey, Put," he said, "howdy partner, I'm going up to surprise Maxine. Got a nice box of candy for me? Good as you got. I ain't got much else to carry."

Putney would never forget those words of Harry's.

If it was a bad turn and a bad year for Putney, it was a bad year for Harry too. And also for Maxine, as one could imagine. Harry, after the quick celebration and a hundred stories taking all kinds of shapes, the dark and the doomed, filled with odd characters and fairy people, ogres and demons of all measures and reaches, drank from one end of the day to the other. For a whole year he didn't pick up a hammer or a saw. Maxine once in a while would come into the store with a puffy lip, or a tear in her eye. Put had to look away, mind his own business, fall out of love if he could, for beyond all things that mattered it was a hopeless situation. She was hurting and Put stopped looking at her the way he had for those few years of his dependence on her.

The story that made the rounds was indeed bizarre, if anything more bizarre than war can be, and rescue at the ends of desperation. Harry, it was learned, was pulled from the Mediterranean by a French fisherman and hidden in the fisherman's house. For a long while he was tucked away in a secret space in the attic of the fisherman's house, where, through one small opening above an eave he could watch the small village square as it revolved under the war and under Nazi occupation. One hellacious day he saw the Germans execute three American fliers right in the square and saw their bodies dropped into a hole, doused with gasoline, and torched. When the fire died out, the remains were covered over at the end of the day, interred right in the square of the little village. Three days later, when house searches were renewed by the Germans, the fisherman moved Harry to another house and a secret room whose access was halfway down the depth of an old well in the cellar. That "hole in the wall" led to a spacious room dug into the hillside many years earlier for a different cause. The new "landlord" had a daughter, Yvette, just 17, who shined on Harry and visited him at least once a week and often stayed most of the night. When she became pregnant, it was apparent the family wanted to keep Harry under cover for as long as they could. Yvette gave birth to a son, and Harry was kept in the room some months after the war was over before he climbed out one night and made his escape.

He fled his European life.

But, as one must realize, the memories of Yvette, and the memory of another son, never quite left Harry. Maxine never admitted to knowing, but she must have known some of the mystery. Harry's long incarceration, the visitations of his young lover, the subsequent son, all hounded him no end. All of it had followed him home to Maxine and the two boys and the subsequent nightly visits, away from home, to bar after frivolous bar, to friend after frivolous friend. The pattern was constant and unbreakable and the deadly inroads were open.

We did not hear the stories come up as spoken history here in town; they drifted in on their own feet, on an everywhichway wind from odd sources coming across town lines by postmen, taxi drivers, delivery men, the coal man Merv Takens who thought Harry should be hospitalized because he had flown on that same flight of alcohol. Problems knocking at Harry's heels were openly discussed in the barber shop, the post office, and in our own bars, though never in the ear of Harry on his way back to the house after a night on the next town, or the one beyond that. After a while we could picture him being followed, ghostlike, by his French lover and mother of his son, and the son himself. That had to be a bear to carry on one's back already borne to drop weights easier than promises.

One night, the moon behind a sudden cloud, mist rising as from the earth the way fog walks on water and roadways and intemperate reaches, history making new demands, life itself asking for settlements, Harry was killed as he walked across the turnpike from one bar

The Storekeeper

to the next, going from John's Bar to Ma Taylor's Kitchen across Route One. One of his own drinking buddies ran him down, never seeing him on the dark road, never seeing the dark specters stepping right out behind his drinking pal, never seeing those who were keeping Harry company.

Putney, to his everlasting credit, started all over. And I watched him again, from a new perspective and a new awareness, only this time he must have measured time and what had been eaten up of that which had been granted to him in the first place. For he picked up some speed in his delivery, like he was coming right out of the bullpen at Fenway Park.

One night a few months later he carried with him his best box of candy and Maxine opened the door for him. Putney the storekeeper shifted directly into second gear. Nothing was ever the same again.

* * *

massachusetts, usa

The Rig Runner

For a pure moment trucker Rene Destot had felt above it all, above dawn at its tatters, above the voice coming at him from day's edge. King of the throne he was, king of the hill, the road having slammed under him all night long. The 475 horses loose in the truck's Caterpillar engine sounded their endless music, hummed under his seat bottom, talked lightly to his wrists. (Controlled rampage, the voice had said long before he used to think

233

about owning a Kenworth, Earth-mover, star-hauler.) House-big, highly modified for cruising, a Caddy in a sense, the Kenworth T2000 went over the crown of the hill. He froze on the edge of the seat.

Had the voice had been talking about this? Night has justice. Day has none. What curve in the road?

Gray skies to the north were releasing massive shapes, taking on lesser ones. Night was crawling away on hands and knees. Rene, not yet bleary-eyed, knew the thievery of it, the moment, the uncertain reigns of clarity that can fall into one's hands as night departs. In obstinate pieces the pre-dawn had been talking to him in the scary way it manifests intonations. Some days pass easily. This one will not. Hearken. Night is a beginning and an end. Even knowing it was his own voice did not make it any more reflective. He had heard it before, sometimes operatic, then in whispers, but not on the road.

Never before on the road. Not behind the wheel. The road, with a justice all its own, has a demand all its own.

Now, in that clarity at hand, sudden sunlight scattered ammunition out there on the road in front of him, sudden flares of chrome flashing in every direction. About another day he thought, odd and rampant shrapnel loose at dawn, detonation and combustion everywhere, decisions at hand, Sgt. Rumney at his feet and crying, metal from their own high angle devils still burning its way through his body. A scant 50 or 60 yards ahead of him a car was broadside in the road, the sun almost breaking down the catalogue of the vehicle's parts. And though there was apparently room on either side for safe passage of the rig, he thought his tires would take an unnecessary beating.

He identified a '98 Crown Victoria, slammed the gears in downshift, feeling the weight pushing at his back, popping the rig towards a slow-down, the gears abruptly humming their mesh of music, just like the back row of the orchestra at a Copland night at Symphony Hall. Forces, as always, were all around him. It was like stopping the world to get off, some kind of carousel, centrifugal. Remembering a French horn destroying a note one night deep in his past made him think about the way the crew packed the load back at

235

The Rig Runner

Swanton's Ridge, not at perfection, thinking it might start shifting, daring to stand on its feet, threatening to jackknife. Then he saw the woman step from behind the car and dart to the side of the road. In his mind was the converse turmoil of a lady in distress and the cost of new truck tires. There was feeble juxtaposition to contend with.

The rig slid by the left side of the Crown Victoria. Gravel and shoulder waste and perimeter-loose asphalt and pebbles sang under his wheels, pinged away as if from a hundred slingshots and he could feel the rig momentarily hang in the air. The woman, young, trim, hair proud-red and like a ball of fire, was waving at him as he veered by. For scant seconds the trailer, potentially a deserter, AWOL in promise, tugged at his backside. From his lungs a pocket of air came loose with a bang. Gears shutting down into lowest low, the cargo still threatening movement, morning suddenly full of other energies, the huge Kenworth and its attachment came to a stop.

In the side mirror the woman was waving at him. The voice, talking again, was unheard.

236

Dropping down from the cab, the demanding rigors of the road fully in his mind and having been in worse spots, he checked the tires on his side. He walked back to the young woman and the car. She was not in panicsville, though her cheeks were flared red. Instantly, with a quiet daring, her eyes measured his eyes, the depth in them, the span of his shoulders, his hipline, the bleached impact of his worn but neat jeans. Rene, at 37, slim and rugged from a decent regimen and a usual tussle with weights, even out on the road, was aware he had certain attractions. Ease, supposedly, was one of them.

"Will the engine start?" he said, looking at the crown of the hill he had just come over. She was trimmer than he thought at first.

"No. Just died on me," she said. One shoulder shrugged. "There's been trouble with it the last few days." The shoulder shrug was the universal one, her head tipping to meet it, eyes shifting color. Her legs were marvelous. She looked clean as a new napkin, but her eyes darker at the moment.

The Rig Runner

"You watch for traffic," Rene said. "I'll try to get it out of the road." Noting her slimness again, how her red hair glossed against her neck, he advised, "Wave something. A sweater, a pocketbook, anything. Wave something."

He dropped into the seat, kept the door open, and keyed the starter. The engine coughed and jerked and he did it a second time. He tried it again and popped the gear quickly into neutral after catching a minor thrust from the starter, and with one foot pushing got the Crown Victoria rolling on a slight grade and coasted it off the road.

"I can give you a lift down to Crawford. It's about twenty miles. There's a garage there. Probably help you out."

"That's great. Let me get my bags. Only a couple." Her eyes, chameleons at work, were as green as a lagoon ought to be. She spun away with a youthful twist, energy riding off her frame. Other forces, the voice said, are about.

Back on the road, the Caterpillar touching him in the wrists again, in the seat of his pants, Rene caught her from the corner of his eye. He knew she was identifying the music on the radio, low and quiet. Her legs were remarkably elegant, even, he thought, for the cab seat of a Kenworth. He'd saved for eight years for the rig, elegance itself, and here was more elegance sitting in his cab than he had ever dreamed of.

"That's lovely," she said. " That's Nessum Dorma and I'm Lila Endwell." Musically she said it. "I was heading home to Ossipee, to see my family. From college. I teach, a half professor. Do you always play that kind of music when you're driving?" Lila Endwell had turned to face him. Her eyes he caught first, now of another hue, not lagoon green, not as dark as earlier, and then her mouth. He could taste her mouth, the serious red lips. It was in his eyes.

"You're blushing. I like that kind of honesty in a man. If you screw up, you screw up. That's really charming, courageous, and extremely sexy. Oh, my brother Tim says I'm too damned direct, but life's too short to be otherwise. Things need doing. My father is godawful overprotective, now, but he's the one should watch out for himself. Thinks he owns half the world and wants the other half. It's going to kill him. I tell him he'll be sorely missed, but that's only a mere caution."

"What's he do?"

"He owns."

"That simple?"

"That much and that simple. If you're going on to Boston, we'll be going right by his place. A long ride by. It's like a border, like you need a passport."

"Your mother?"

"The owning killed her. I got out. I still love him, in some way, but I got out. She worked forever for him, at anything, and when she wasn't there any more, neither was I. She used to slip into my room at night, barefoot, smelling nice, and tell me stories. Sometimes she kept me up looking at the stars, the moon, telling me stories her mother had told her. About witches and sadness and losing the moon when you wanted it most. And he was downstairs doing the books. We knew the

240

difference, and the parting. We all parted before we knew it. As a kid it was all done. Before she died it was all done. Can you reach something like that?"

"Yes. If you're looking for something besides the trucker response, I'll find it for you." He could have harrumped, but let it go. "I guess it's like notes in music that come up in one place but you know they belong someplace else. Only if you really listen, nothing else in your mind, absolutely no taste in your mouth, no beauty in your eye, nothing to touch. Even the composer never knew it. All things aren't what they always seem. My pal Eddie drives a Diamond-T and he knows every damn word of Gilbert and Sullivan. Every damn word."

"That's wild! I'm sorry for the unintended aspersion. Are you a composer? A Musician? A music buff? Love Country and Western? Blues besides the longhair? Where does Jazz fit itself, on an edge?" Each of them realized that she could go on much longer, but was being temperate, allowing her eyes to change again.

"You keep talking like that and I'll remember you a long way down the road."

241

The Rig Runner

"Oh, you'll remember my good legs and thinking about the oral stuff, the way you guys do. What do they say, every five or six seconds? My God, how can you drive? I think it comes with the equipment, doesn't it? Part of the spec sheet? Au naturel. My God, I'd be running all the red lights!" He realized there was not an edge to her voice. It was the way she talked, so utterly natural. And for kicks the air caught a small grasp of a new aroma, an essence of personal identification, more than newly cut grass or a vast salty marsh or a whole mountain cleansed just after rain. It said, for that moment and forever, Lila Endwell. He didn't know if he had said her name or the voice had said her name. He pretended ignorance.

"Head on and no red lights?" His thumb hit a switch on the wheel and Eddie Arnold, somewhere in a corner of the huge sleeper cab, was about as sad as one can get, the kind of song Sgt. Rumney had played and leaned on all the time.

"I like Country. I like him. It's what the traffic bears, but no adjusting of personality. I like myself sometimes. I love my father, I guess, but I don't like him. I liked my mother and loved her, barefoot, smelling nice, the moon in the window like colored glass. I think already I like you. You come this way often? Where from? Where to?"

"I'll go by three more times in the next week and a half." He looked at a small calendar on the visor. "Then maybe not again for three or four months."

"Will you blow that crazy horn, if you have one, when you go by?"

"Sure."

"I'd rather you stopped and knocked at the door, if you could manage it."

"What would your father say with this rig at his door?"

"All he has to dictate is his will, and I think he's done that by now. I'm on my own, up to my own. The critters in my puddle are the ones I float with." She popped fully sideways in the seat. "You're coming back this way, right?"

Her knees shone at the back of his eyes, a field of white, expansive, compelling. If he saw much more of her, he'd explode. "Tomorrow, back over the same route."

"Let's drop in, say hello, get the car squared away, and then I'll go to Boston with you. I'll treat you to dinner. I'm on vacation."

He understood the aegis of her argument. "I won't leave the truck for very long. And never in the city if I can help it. The investment is enormous." If he ever needed the voice, now was the time.

"Then we'll party here. After, you can bring me back home, and when you leave you can blow that crazy horn." Standing up beside the seat, she slipped into the back of the cab. In half a yodel she said, "Hell--o." There should have been an echo. "It's like a damn gymnasium back here. I saw you looking," she said. It was not coy. Did not come across that way. "There's nothing but silk under there. Nothing but silk."

...They had stopped, met her father. She kissed her father after showering, steered Rene out the door, left her father on the huge porch in the exhaust of the Kenworth, in its shade. His shoulders were slumped. Rene, remembering later, swore he could hear her mother telling a story in three rooms, in the huge hallway, in the dining room, in the den where they had a glass of wine. It was another voice, at least.

His cargo was delivered, a new load put on for a return trip. There was dinner for two outside the city. A few glasses of wine. Later, a bottle of Madeira she took from a small case she brought with her. They made love in the Kenworth cab, parked in a rest area with a dozen other trucks holed up for the night. Rene Destot fell in love after they made love, after she showed him there was nothing but silk under there. "It's the wave of the future," she said. "It's our call," as she explained how she shaved herself. He shivered.

He was in Vergennes, outbound, when he found the suitcase on the lower bunk under a pillow and blanket. The neat blocks of currency were piled like Leggos in the case. He counted to a million and fifty thousand. There was no note, but he could smell her, like he could hear a high note left on the air.

The Rig Runner

When he drove back to the mansion, the police were there. There was noise, static, the sound of sirens. One trooper told him a woman had killed her rich father, and then herself. "No note," he said. "Strange, you have to admit. Had everything going for them. Or so it seemed." His voice was distant, like coming down a long tunnel, night behind it, pushing for all it was worth.

It all came back. Some days pass easily. This one will not. Night is a beginning and an end.

* * *

gujarat, india

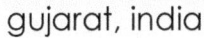

Photo: Deepack

Bhadauria Manish Singh

gujarat, india

Bhadauria Manish Singh was born on 3rd December 1982 at Ahmedabad in Gujarat. He is a poet and Short Story writer. Right now he is pursuing his doctorate on the Indian English Poetry of Jayanta Mahapatra from J.J.T University Rajasthan.

He has published his short stories and poems in numerous literary magazines and journals like Indian Rumination, Nazar Look, Tajmahal Review and Harvest of New Millennium. He has also presented his research papers at more than twenty national and international conferences. He published his first poetry collection called "World: Inner and Outer" in 2012 published by Cyberwit.net.

The Lunatic

It was around 5 'O clock, stars have already surrendered to morning sun rays. As usual, it was chilly and windy. The whole city was still in the lap of the winter sleep, but few day dreamers and not so physically perfect people were out in their quest to get perfection. Then a group of dogs broke the blessed silence in their growls and war cries, nothing new but their eternal clash for areas and females. I kept walking in hope to lose some inches. Again it was calm, serene and silent but it lasted all too short as it was now human mass who broke the silence. Just at the entrance of the garden, few were beating a man; he was clad in tattered and muddy clothes. He had a long black beard and an untidy, unearthly bag. Frankly just out of curiosity I interrupted and inquired. I came to know: the so called lunatic fellow had harassed a beautiful woman on her morning walk, and who want to miss such a chance to beat the villain and be a hero? That man holding his

The Lunatic

bag tightly was trying to say something. He looked so frightened, he was bleeding. At last he fainted, and now it was the time for the crowd to get frighten. They all ran helter and skelter, thinking he might be dead. I was also about to go, but he moaned and stretched towards his bag. I stopped thought for a while, about police, formalities, hospital bill etc and etc but at last called an ambulance. I had to go to the hospital to complete the formalities. I was sitting in the waiting lounge of the government hospital and thinking, "Why have I spoiled my Sunday, my walk for a lunatic who harassed a beautiful woman? How villainous this is!" Doctor came and interrupted my musings. He told me that I could meet him. I went inside, and told him to not to do such things in future. He remained calm and then all of a sudden asked about his bag. I was furious and puzzled, I told him, "We had left his bag outside the garden on a bench." The fellow joined in his both hands and pleaded with tears to fetch the bag for him. I was in no mood to do him any favour but there was something which made me agree at last. I reached garden taking a rickshaw, and no surprise his bag was still there. It was his bag's unearthly condition which saved it from others beggars and even from dogs. I looked all around to see whether anybody was watching me doing that. Finally I did it and took the same auto again for the hospital. I had no courage to peep inside that bag. I reached and handed over the thing to the person. But he was in no mood to spare my Sunday, he asked me to stop. He asked me to come close, I obeyed. He gave me a photo, being a student of literature I recognized the person in the photo. It was the photo of Professor Sameer Mehta, who used to teach in one of the reputed colleges of the Ahmedabad city. I saw him in one of the seminars attended by me a long back. I asked him, "What he has to do with Professor Mehta?" He smiled and said, "I have everything to do with him. I am Professor Mehta." I could see the truth in his eyes and closely watched him and photograph, yes he was right. I had a lot of questions but before I could ask something he had asked me. He asked my name and my profession. He was more than happy to know that I was struggling to publish my first short story book. He asked me to call nurse and make him sit. I did that and with more happiness now. For a start I asked him, "Sir, how could you and how did you, and how can you live like this?" Again instead of replying anything he orders me to bring a pen and paper, for writing. I gave paper and pen to him. He handed it back to me and said, "Do you want to have a new story?" I nodded, "then write". He started to narrate;

People used to know me as Professor Sameer Mehta and now no one knows me except those people in that garden, who thrashed me and yes my so called victim too. I am a lunatic a bloody psycho or maniac. But let me tell you the reason for this transgression...no...actually an upliftment. One has to remember while running in the race for success that it will be futile if you don't have your close ones to share and celebrate it. I am taking this opportunity to deliver my final lecture my own story.

"I don't have much time now, so I begin, from where it actually began. I was 21, doing my masters in English, Sarita was in my class. I can't say it was the love at first sight. But something was there in her which attracted me towards her from the first day. It all began usually as it happens with exchanging notes and then phone numbers and address. In her I found, what I always lacked in my life. I was the only son of my widowed mother and Sarita was the daughter of a mill worker. So there was no gulf of caste and wealth between us as it usually happens in love here. This fact catalyzed our bond, and soon we became first really close friends. We know each other more than our own selves. We could understand each other's silence and fake smiles. We both aimed high, to secure good life for our family. Yes, it was not purely a love of literature which made me professor, it was the necessities also. As I was weak in Maths, after passing twelfth science in second class I didn't go for B. SC instead opted B.A English. Sarita was the real support and guide; she was much more clear and mature in her way towards life. Her companionship made me responsible and mature. We both passed out with first class. Then came a dark phase in her life she surrendered her studies as her father passed away. She started working as a teacher and played the role of her father for his mother and two brothers. I was in no condition to help her. I also got busy in preparation for clearing National Eligibility examination to become a Professor. In spite of over burden, she kept on helping me. She used to come at my

The Lunatic

home frequently to help me in my studies. She kept awake with me, prepared notes for me. My mother also started treating her like her *Bahu**. And one night when my mother was away with some relatives in a marriage, we crossed the limits. Rather I crossed the limits, she protested, denied but then surrendered out of her love for me. But after that day, she stopped coming by night. She used to come but at the day time, only when my mother was around. It was nothing like that, she was angry...actually she didn't want me to distract myself from my aim. And then hers, mine and our family's prayer got heard at last. I passed NET with flying colors. We were more than happy. Then came the day on which I got my job as Professor at a girl's college at Gandhinagar. I got a compartment there, we shifted from Ahmedabad. I came to visit her on every weekend. Friend, it is hard to achieve success and believe me it is much harder to digest it. I could not digest it; I got busy in my PhD, in my new upgraded life, my new female colleagues, new house then new car. I kept on climbing stairs up and up, she was left behind. I didn't grab her hand. I started ignoring her, giving her excuses for not meeting. She never complained, but I knew in some corner of my heart that I was doing wrong. I was in a kind of addiction to success. Years passed and one day came the news that she was dying from cancer. I still remember the day my mother came in room and slapped me hard to give that news. It was as if somebody has drenched me with cold water, the hangover of the success begin to disappear. But it was too late, she was trying to inform me but I was too busy in my own success. I went to meet her at the hospital, she just kept me staring. She gave me a tiny box having sindoor* in it and asked me to apply it between her brows. I did it and it all ended like a sad love story. She was gone for ever without any complain, and my guilt started eating me. I decide to not to marry any one else, my mother also went one day forever into another world, leaving me behind with my alienation. And then I sold my whole property and given a half portion of it to her family via a trust of my friend and half I have given as a charity to the cancer hospital. I left the college, my home too but guilt never left me. I could have saved her. I could have given her more joy; I should not have hurt her so much. People thought I am a lunatic; but I can see her all around me. She just comes and stares me for hours, she don't talk to me. In garden I was chasing her. Still she is here only, look at there near the gate."

I turned my head towards the gate and found nothing. I again turned my face towards professor...but there was only his body. May be now he was with his Sarita...I opened his bag and found a box containing few old letters and notes perhaps written by Sarita for Sameer and I also found their photos. I also found a letter declaring his last wish. He wanted to donate his body to Medical College. I called the doctor and completed the formalities.

I just want to say we can be luckier than Sameer, if we realize our mistakes before cancer of relationship. We should awake from slumber before anybody has to slap us. I request all the Sameers who have forgotten their Saritas in their race for success. As Professor had said, "Every success is incomplete if you don't have the one to share and celebrate for it."

Notes

Bahu- Indian Word for Daughter-in-law
Sindoor- Indian word for Vermilion, applied by Husband between burrows of her Wife as a ritual during Hindu Marriage

british columbia, canada

Photo: Anna Whitlock

Hollis Whitlock

british columbia, canada

Tantra Bensko **CARLY BERG** *Ute Carson* TONY CONCANNON Rudy Ch. Garcia
Margaret Karmaz

Hollis Whitlock lives and writes in Vancouver BC.

He has four children and a wife.

He coaches T-ball and volunteers for a newspaper.

Margaret Karmazin JAMES D. REED W. Jack Savage **Tom**
MANISH SINGH Hollis Whitlock SAMUEL K. WILKES Abigail Wyatt
Berg Ute Carson Rudy Ch. Garcia **MARGARET KARMAZIN**
ED W. JACK SAVAGE Tom Sheehan Bhadauria Manish Singh
muel K. Wilkes ABIGAIL WYATT Tantra Bensko Carly Berg Ute
Margaret Karmazin JAMES D. REED W. Jack Savage TOM
nish Singh Hollis Whitlock SAMUEL K. WILKES Abigail Wyatt TANTRA
g Ute Carson Tony Concannon Rudy Ch. Garcia JAMES D. REED W.
Sheehan BHADAURIA MANISH SINGH Hollis Whitlock Samuel K.
Tantra Bensko CARLY BERG Ute Carson Tony Concannon Rudy
Karmazin W. Jack Savage TOM SHEEHAN Bhadauria Manish
LOCK Samuel K. Wilkes Abigail Wyatt TANTRA BENSKO Carly Berg UTE
cannon Rudy Ch. Garcia Margaret Karmazin JAMES D. REED Tom
MANISH SINGH Hollis Whitlock SAMUEL K. WILKES Abigail
Carly Berg Ute Carson TONY CONCANNON Rudy Ch. Garcia
JAMES D. REED W. Jack Savage Bhadauria Manish Singh HOLLIS
K. Wilkes ABIGAIL WYATT Tantra Bensko Carly Berg UTE
RUDY CH. GARCIA Margaret Karmazin JAMES D. REED W.
eehan Hollis Whitlock SAMUEL K. WILKES Abigail Wyatt
Carly Berg Ute Carson TONY CONCANNON Rudy Ch. Garcia MARGARET
S D. REED W. Jack Savage Tom Sheehan Bhadauria Manish Singh
IGAIL WYATT Tantra Bensko CARLY BERG Ute Carson Tony
H. GARCIA Margaret Karmazin JAMES D. REED W. Jack Savage
Tom Sheehan Bhadauria Manish Singh Hollis Whitlock Abigail Wyatt TANTRA BENSKO
Carly Berg UTE CARSON Tony Concannon Rudy Ch. Garcia MARGARET KARMAZIN JAMES
D. REED W. JACK SAVAGE Tom Sheehan Bhadauria Manish Singh Hollis Whitlock Samuel

258

The Search for Eternal Life

$John$ struggled to lean against the headboard of his cot. He looked through the window at the pristine grounds of his estate. He had imported exotic trees, shrubs, and perennials from around the world. Numerous magazines had featured the gardens. Local clubs had praised the floral displays. Thirty years of planting, fertilizing and sculpting had transformed the once barren landscape into a paradise that he called home.

John turned and coughed excessively into a white handkerchief. Thin strands of gray shifted over his wrinkled forehead. He combed them back over his discolored scalp with his fingers and peered at Mary's watery eyes.

"Have a drink," Mary said, handing him a crystal glass that contained a mixture of pure cranberry juice, hand squeezed lemon juice and carbonated spring

259

water. John spat into the hanky and wiped the phlegm from his mouth. His eyes were squinted red pools of tears. His face was withered like a man twenty years his age. His voice crackled in-between coughing gasps.

"Thank you," John replied.

"It's almost time for your treatment."

"It's not helping. It's making me feel worse. I've had enough."

Doctors had diagnosed John's cancer three month ago. Numerous scans, blood tests, needle extractions, and bodily samples had revealed that his bladder and liver contained numerous tumors. Practitioners of medicine had given him four to six months to live, but the malignant tumors were rapidly metastasizing.

"The doctors will be here shortly."

"Send them away. I want to prepare for the afterlife in peace."

"Alright, I'll tell them that you've past."

"Yes, I have some thoughts that I'd like to discuss with you before I go."

Mary smiled and hugged John's frail body. Tears ran from two sets of eyes. They had married thirty years ago after graduating from university. John had worked as a scientist in the discipline of parapsychology. Mary was a psychiatric nurse. They'd bought the property in a rural district after three year's employment and renovated the house with credit and savings. John wheezed painfully and leaned back.

"I'm going to miss you, but I'm sure you're going to a better place."

"How can I be going to a better place than this? This is where I want to be. I want to spend the rest of our lives together."

"So do I John." Mary's face was sullen. "I wish there was something I could do."

"There might be. What if I'm going to reincarnate? Maybe somewhere close by. You could leave some sort of message that would remind me." Mary smiled mournfully and wiped the sweat from John's forehead with a damp cloth.

"You've lived a clean healthy life. I'm sure we'll be reunited in heaven."

"Heaven? I have that here with you."

"That's what I thought too John, but the lord is calling. There must be a greater need for you somewhere else."

"But I haven't finished my work here. I can't accept that my life's research will be in vain."

"Your work won't be in vain, another young scientist will begin where you've left off."

The Search for Eternal Life

John coughed painfully into his bony hands. Mary wiped his mouth with a moist cloth. Tears streamed down John's cheeks. He eased his rasping throat with a swill of the cold liquid. Mary took the glass and refilled it.

"Not likely. There's little faith in what I'm studying. The scientist would have to be me. No one else understands my work. And most of it's still in my mind, waiting to be scribed onto paper."

"I'm sure the lord will allow you to continue your research in heaven."

"But where is heaven, if it's not here with you? We've flown through the clouds, walked on the moon and scoured the desolate soils of Mars."

"John. Don't be silly."

"There's nothing there. It has to be somewhere here on Earth." A glint of light gleamed from John's eyes like a light bulb turning on. Mary smiled. John's youthful appearance seemed to return. He sat upright and sipped from his glass. "I want you to find my future self and make sure that I continue my studies and that I don't end up on a path of destruction as so many youths do." Mary chuckled.

"And how am I going to do that?"

"There must be a way. Other cultures have done it. Something of this life must be retained. It has to have purpose and meaning or why would we even bother?"

"I've had faith in the lord my entire life, as blind as it may be, but losing you is truly testing me. That's what I believe."

"Do you have faith in me? I'm here for a little while longer."

"John I'll search for you after you're gone if that's what you want, but you'll have to give me some sort of a clue where to look."

John rubbed the gray stubble on his chin and looked down at the bed. He coughed and took a drink. Mary sighed and held his trembling hand. John looked at Mary with a row of fine lines on his forehead. His expression was intense.

"I've estimated that there are three hundred births per day in our city, on average."

"That sounds about right."

"I have to be one of those babies." Mary's eyes pooled with liquid. She blinked twice and wiped her tears. John had always been a man of logic and wisdom. Mary smirked before placing her hand over her mouth. "Mary, I'm serious about this."

"I know you are, but why are you so certain about reincarnation? And can you really round it down to this city?"

"Every religion known to mankind has a form of reincarnation. It's either here on Earth, or in some Holy Land we call heaven and my heaven is here with you."

263

"Well it could be at the time of conception. That's when life starts."

"You're complicating things." John placed his hand over his eyes. "We could never..." Tears streamed down his cheeks onto the pristine white sheets. He looked downward. Mary hugged him and kissed his cheek. Knocking resonated off the front door. "Please send them away."

"I'll be back in moment."

John lay back and closed his eyes. Soft footsteps echoed down the stairs. Two more knocks disturbed his peace. A creaking door opened. Saddened voices were muffled. The door slammed closed. Footsteps hastened up the stairs. John sighed heavily and drifted off. He felt a warm hand on his forehead.

"John. Are you still there? I've sent them away."

"Yes, I'm still here. I'm trying to find my future being. My past and future is somewhere locked within my subconscious. It's just a matter of finding it." Mary rubbed her forehead and glanced at the clock on the wall.

"Your past certainly is, but I don't know about the future."

"If I can go backward, why can't I go forward?"

"The past has happened and the memories are stored within your mind, but the future is uncertain. It has yet to happen. We can make plans and decisions and then change them at the last moment."

"Yes, but if I follow through on those plans then the outcome is known. I have control over my destiny."

"John we had plans for the future, but the lord has changed them. I'm as disappointed as you are. I have to go on alone."

"Mary at least humor me. I'm certain I've lived a past life. There has to be something that I brought with me into this life."

"John I remember your mother and father. They gave you a fantastic upbringing."

"It's not just that. Could we try some hypnosis again? I was so close last time."

"Sure we can try again."

Mary breathed deeply and picked up her father's antique pocket watch. Its subtle ticking kept perfect time like a healthy heart. It was made of the finest materials and encased in silver. Sunlight gleamed off its brushed nickel surface onto the wall. John shifted awkwardly on the bed.

"Would you place another pillow under my head?" Mary grabbed a cushion and helped John lean forward. She placed it under his upper back and head. "That's better. My body aches all the time. In a way I'll be glad to get out of here." Mary wiped her eyes and sat

The Search for Eternal Life

on the bed. She held the watch up. A halo formed above John's head.

"Where shall we start?"

"Down by the stream at the back of the property where we used to go for walks. Did you carve the inscription on the glacial boulder?"

"Yes I did."

"Ok, I want to see if I can read it."

Mary smiled while swinging the watch gently back and forth. Her voice was soft and soothing as she spoke. John closed his eyes and visualized her words.

* * *

Humid air, from the misting sky, filled his lungs, as he jogged toward the stream. Along the trail, murky pools of water had formed in crevices of protruding roots and sharp stones. He stumbled periodically with the shifting of gravel, but maintained his balance, as his bare feet left imprints of a child. Mud oozed between his toes.

Ahead, clouds of fog, drifting from the decaying underbrush, hid the trail. He stopped to pick the odd berry that still clung to the stem. A dash of sweet, almost sickly liquid moistened his tongue's palate. Seeds ground into his molars before rasping down his throat. His eyes searched for more.

The gardens gleamed with vivid color like the Saturday morning's cartoons, but faded to almost black and white with a darkening gust of wind and then back to color with another warming gust. Birds chirped while darting from branch to branch. Running water reverberated from ahead.

"Well I think that's enough...I'm going to..."

"No, no I'm almost there. It's as clear as day. I'm just about at the stream. Please continue." Mary smiled warmly.

"Alright. If it makes you happy."

He walked to the bank of the stream, beneath the towering evergreens, four feet above the water and peered downward. Salmon were spawning around the jagged rocks in the shallow rapids. Many lay motionless on the gravel on the edge of the stream. Seagulls and crows pecked incessantly at the skeletal remains. Logs and branches lay across the river creating motionless patches in the stream's flow.

He slid down the bank on the soft peat moss to the edge. A three-foot salmon, which was blurred to pastel red, green and black, by the flowing water, hovered just below the surface. Numerous lacerations were across its back. Bits of torn skin exposed pink flesh along its flank.

A smaller salmon lay trapped between two boulders below him. Hundreds of pink eggs were scattered on the gravel. The bigger salmon wriggled against the current. Creamy white clouded the waters.

The Search for Eternal Life

"Are you going to return to the ocean?"

A sudden writhe propelled the salmon out of the current. Water splashed upward speckling his face with a chill. An eye glared from the salmon's brilliant red head. Razor sharp teeth protruded from a hooked snout. A calm voice spoke.

"No. I've completed my life's cycle."

"But there is so much more to see and do." A second splash sent more droplets onto his face. He wiped them with the sleeve of his shirt. The lifeless salmon drifted downstream, twisting and turning against the rocks, boulders, and branches. More flesh tore loose. He watched for a moment, wanting to help, and then ran along the stream's shore in pursuit. "Wait!"

He stopped running when he noticed a salmon gasping on the shoreline. Its red gills were wide open. An eye was twirling in a circle. Pink eggs were scattered in the calm water beside him. Three gulls hopped closer.

"Can you step on me?"

"What?"

"Step on me. I can't do it myself. It's my last hope." His heal squished into the soft decaying flesh. A spray of white speckled the stream's surface and then clouded the water. "Thank you." The circling eye stopped and stared directly at him.

"You're welcome."

He walked farther along the trail to a bridge where the stream flowed at a much greater pace. Salmon were leaping from the river, just beneath his grasp, up the steep incline, next to the glacial boulder. Finger scribed lines were carved on its moss surface.

"Mary, I'm by the boulder."

"I'm glad you've found it."

"I'm trying to read what it says. Don't tell me. I know I can do this."

"I'm not going to tell you."

"If only I had more time. I could prove this can be done."

"You're not gone yet John."

He placed his hand on the dampness of the moss and shifted in front of the lettering. Misting rain had displaced portions of the greenery, but the message was decipherable. The inscription read: I'm scattering your ashes down by the inlet where the salmon gather before spawning.

"I'm going to see if you're there. Then I can leave you a message where to find me."

"Alright John let's continue."

"I'm in the future Mary. I know it."

He sprinted down the slope, along the winding trail, past the ancient evergreens until glimpses of rippling blue encompassed the horizon. The trail narrowed and sloped downward to a rock formation that led to the inlet. He carefully scaled the slippery surface to the water's edge. Salmon were feeding on herring. Gulls were hovering in white patches above the ocean's surface.

A lure landed fifty feet away amongst a school of salmon. Two small hands reeled quickly on the line. A red and white bobber floated on the choppy ocean's surface before suddenly submerging into the depths.

"Mom, mom I've caught a fish." A woman dressed in black holding an urn turned to her son's voice. She saw John's spirit in the child's ebullience and tossed the ashes into the sea.

"You can rest in peace John. I still have a part of you."

* * *

Photo: Dan Anderson

Samuel K. Wilkes

alabama, usa

Samuel Wilkes is a thirty-year old attorney, writer, and musician living on the Eastern Shore of Mobile Bay, Alabama with his wife, Libba, and plump wiener dog, Gus.

His short fiction has been published in the Steel Toe Review, Crack The Spine (Issue #59), Wordland 3 and Mod Mobilian Press' print anthology Tributaries 2012. His short story "Missing the Point" is scheduled to appear in the WhiskeyPaper around August of 2013.

Leaving the Nest

They did not know he had reached his last night. One rarely does. They knew it was coming though. His hair had faded to grey. The steps took longer to climb. Energy came in spurts but fizzled quickly like a wind-up toy.

"Kathy. Give him some," Carl said, eyeing her and eyeing him.

She tore off a piece of her dinner roll and handed it to him. His sensitive teeth pressed into the baked flour.

"Talked to Jason today," Kathy offered the room.

"Is he coming home for Thanksgiving?"

Leaving the Nest

"No, remember I already told you."

Carl looked down at Hamlet then back up at Kathy.

"He's going to some concert up in Nashville. I don't know. He acted like it was a big deal. I didn't argue with him."

Carl pushed his hamburger steak around the plate like a hockey puck.

"I think it's a girl," Kathy said, almost at a whisper, as if letting Hamlet in on a secret.

"Hell, I hope so. Better than him being on drugs—or worse!"

The clock struck 8:30 p.m. as the chimes filled the empty hallway.

Kathy picked up her plate, "Don't worry, I'll get the dishes tonight."

Carl slid on his pullover and boots—the same pullover and boots that had sat by the door ready for the daily routine since he retired. The Millers had a small fenced in back patio with some shrubs and grass, but Carl preferred to walk Hamlet around the front and back yard on a leash, allowing him to take in the smells of the squirrels, the pecans, the bay, and the scant evidence of the stealthy deer that whispered in and out of the neighborhood at dusk. Carl knew this was the highlight of their son's day, and was gradually coming to admit it was his as well.

Hamlet's grey legs stepped slowly down the brick steps. His wet nose pivoted on the fall air. Carl tightened the leash and relit his cigar. The flame pulsed through the black screen of the rural night. Hamlet barked at unknown movement in the adjacent wooded lot. It could have been a raccoon or an armadillo or a possum—could have been a lot of things—only Hamlet knew. His sense of smell was still strong in his older years. He marched forward, proving to his Paw that he still had it, that he was willing to face the darkness in protection of his family as he had always volunteered to do.

"It's ok now, buddy. Let's go over here," Carl said calmly, directing him away from the wooded lot.

Leaving the Nest

The metal clasp of the leash jangled in the hushed night. Hamlet selected his spots to mark with particular precision. Steam rose from the cold ground with each lift of his leg. Hamlet lost his balance as a loud motorcycle growled down the street. He charged at the commotion, barking with an unyielding passion as if a grizzly were clawing at their den. Carl smiled and watched his son behind the thick smoke of his cigar.

* * *

"Where's my baby? Come see your momma!" Kathy called from the couch.

Hamlet lapped up some water from his bowl in the kitchen. He did not hear her voice, but wagged his tail into the den nonetheless, knowing this was that time of the night. Kathy helped him onto the couch. He sprawled out atop the blanket and licked the hairless patch of skin on his leg.

"Did you see that cat?" she asked as if expecting a reply. "Was she out there prancing around?"

Kathy stroked the top of his head and ears, releasing endorphins. Carl sat down after pouring a bourbon drink. He smiled at his family from across the room as if beholding a portrait.

"Has Sadie called?"

On cue, the telephone rang before his wife could answer.

"Her ears must've been burning," Kathy said excitedly, dropping her reading glasses over her eyes and looking at the caller ID. She answered, "Hey, girl, just talking about you."

Carl watched his wife of forty years catching up with their daughter. He watched Hamlet watch her hand as she motioned out her words and fiddled with her rings.

"Well, are y'all going to see his family on Thanksgiving then?"

Carl rattled the ice in his glass.

"Well that's understandable...sure...sure...no, of course not, that's fine, sweetie. We'll see y'all some time...yep, Hamlet's right here licking his leg," she removed the phone from her ear, "Sadie says 'hello' guys."

"Are they not coming?" Carl whispered sharply.

Kathy ignored him and continued on the phone, "Well, no, Jason said he's going to some concert. I am not sure who with...do you know if he's seeing a girl now?"

Hamlet sighed and resituated his head.

"Well, should we be worried about him, Sadie?" Kathy continued.

Carl turned on the television and found a 24-hour news channel.

"Turn it down," Kathy motioned with her hand.

Carl looked to Hamlet knowing he was familiar with the frustration and sympathized.

"Love you too, sweetie. Tell Jim we said Happy Thanksgiving. Bye bye."

"I knew it," he said, taking up his bourbon.

"Well, Carl, we have to learn to share. He has family too you know."

"I guess you could call them that," he huffed.

"Oh, tell your Paw to hush," Kathy said to Hamlet, his chin resting on her knee.

The ice collapsing in Carl's drink could be heard over the muted television. He rose slowly and made them both another cocktail.

* * *

Upon returning, Carl turned the television volume up to one click below a blown speaker. Hamlet was not bothered. They listened to the talking heads read out pithy comments over one another; then glazed over the commercials. Hamlet never turned to the television; he only eyed his parents and occasionally his reflection in the chimney glass screen. He ultimately drifted off to sleep, his back leg kicking in some foreign world where careless squirrels scampered about just waiting to be caught.

Carl looked over smiling, "Isn't it crazy that he knows when you are coming home long before you pull in the driveway?"

"He has senses we can never understand," Kathy said, competing with the yells of a local car dealer.

"What goes through that little ol' head of his?"

"Love," Kathy whispered as if not to wake him.

"Remember when we got him and surprised Jason?"

"Oh, he wanted a dog so bad. I don't think he believed Hamlet was real at first."

"Remember you had him wrapped in a blanket the whole car ride home. Just a little bitty ol' thing," he said, taking a sip of his bourbon.

"Jason kept saying he was going to take him off to college."

"Yea, right."

"Thank the Lord he didn't. Where would we be now?" she smiled and patted his head gently, trying not to wake him.

They both took sips while their minds continued deeper into the warm familiar past. They had had this same conversation many times before, but both willfully came back to it time and time again like putting on a favorite old record. They yearned for that moment in time, when the family they created was all under their roof bustling with life, drama, and love. But they also had accepted that the stages of life keep moving whether you're ready or not. Still, having Hamlet made the nest seem less empty. They cherished him for that and tried to appreciate every moment as the time ticked down.

The clock chimed in the empty hall, waking them from their reflection. Like Pavlov's conditioning, Carl changed the television to the 10 o'clock local news and settled back into the present. Within an hour the entire family had fallen asleep in their usual positions. Carl woke up first by his own chainsaw-like snoring. He sat up startled for a moment, then checked his watch and rose slowly to turn off the lamps. The three slowly progressed to the bedroom like marching penguins. Kathy picked up Hamlet first and placed him on the mattress. He waited at the top until Carl and Kathy finally settled in too. He nosed his way under the covers and burrowed down in between their feet where the warmth concentrated, flanked seamlessly by his parents.

"Love you guys," Carl whispered to his family.

"Love you, honey. And good night, sweet prince," she said softly, reaching below to rub the top of Hamlet's resting head.

* * *

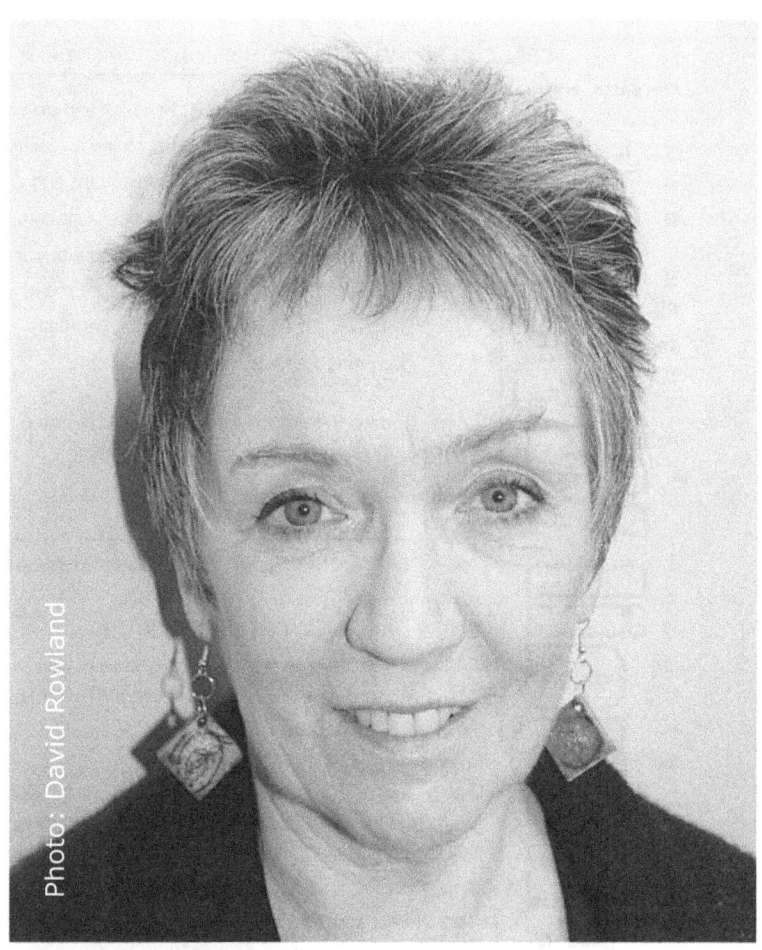

Photo: David Rowland

Abigail Wyatt

england, uk

abigailelizabethwyatt.wordpress.com

Tantra Bensko **CARLY BERG** *Ute Carson* TONY CONCANNON Rudy Ch. Garcia

Margaret Karmaz

Manish Singh Hollis

Tony Concannon RUD

Abigail Wyatt

Abigail Wyatt was born in Orsett in Essex and grew up in the village of Aveley. Before becoming a teacher she worked as a a typist, a nursing assistant and a play leader, did shifts at an all-night petrol station, and sold newspaper advertising. After graduating as a teacher she moved to Cornwall where, for twenty years, she taught at Redruth School, eventually becoming Head of the English Faculty.

She is now a full-time writer and one of the three editors of Poetry24. Her poetry and short fiction, have appeared in more than seventy outlets.

Sheehan BHADAURIA MANISH SINGH Hollis Whitlock **Samuel K.**
TT Tantra Bensko **CARLY BERG** *Ute Carson* Tony Concannon Rudy
Karmazin w. Jack Savage **TOM SHEEHAN** *Bhadauria Manish*
OCK Samuel K. Wilkes **Abigail Wyatt** TANTRA BENSKO Carly Berg UTE
cannon Rudy Ch. Garcia Margaret Karmazin JAMES D. REED Tom
MANISH SINGH *Hollis Whitlock* SAMUEL K. WILKES Abigail
CARLY BERG *Ute Carson* TONY CONCANNON Rudy Ch. Garcia
JAMES D. REED W. Jack Savage Bhadauria Manish Singh **HOLLIS**
K. Wilkes ABIGAIL WYATT Tantra Bensko **Carly Berg** UTE
RUDY CH. GARCIA *Margaret Karmazin* JAMES D. REED W.
eehan Hollis Whitlock **SAMUEL K. WILKES** *Abigail Wyatt*
Carly Berg **Ute Carson** TONY CONCANNON Rudy Ch. Garcia MARGARET
S D. REED W. Jack Savage Tom Sheehan Bhadauria Manish Singh
IGAIL WYATT *Tantra Bensko* CARLY BERG Ute Carson **Tony**
Concannon RUDY CH. GARCIA *Margaret Karmazin* JAMES D. REED W. Jack Savage
Tom Sheehan **Bhadauria Manish Singh** Hollis Whitlock Abigail Wyatt **TANTRA BENSKO**
Carly Berg UTE CARSON Tony Concannon **Rudy Ch. Garcia** MARGARET KARMAZIN JAMES
D. REED W. JACK SAVAGE *Tom Sheehan* Bhadauria Manish Singh Hollis Whitlock Samuel

The Long March Home

Even for me, the heat is oppressive. It must be more than eighty degrees and the air is humid and still. I lie here silenced, hearing the silence, listening for the footfall of the nurses. I am carried along by the ebb and flow of an ocean of delirium and pain. In the wake of each wave, as I struggle for breath, my poor throat swells and closes. Between my empty, shrivelled breasts, sweat collects in a pool.

Here in China the women are like flowers, slender and delicately made. We have small breasts, not

285

ripe and round like the ones so much admired in the West. My own breasts were pale and tipped with fire like the unfolding petals of the lotus. My lover made my nipples sing and my heart beat like the wings of a bird.

This was in the time of Li Yunhe when I thought to find my freedom in the heavens. I was deceived in that. I was a fledgling thing but my aspirations soared. I looked for the safety I had never had and sold myself lightly for a songbird. Instead, it was a poor dumb thing that fell sullen and silent in its cage. So *much* has happened that has brought me here to the end of all my flying. Still, I have slipped through their bars at last and I will not let them cage me again.

In the meantime, the pain threatens. It swells like a wave on the horizon. I must prepare myself as I did in childbirth to straddle its glittering peak. As much as death, *life* is pain: *everything* is sorrow and anguish. Each one of us, woman or man, comes at last to the long march home.

* * *

286

Now I am waking to my other life and the face I peeled away when it suited. My lips are full, rouged and pouting, my eyes sultry and large. My high, arched brows are pencilled in; my skin is pink and translucent. This is the face that my lover loved and my second husband despised. He could not bear that he could not buy what he knew I gave so freely. It ate away at his narrow heart and drove him to madness and despair. There have been those who have blamed and reviled me for it but my face was always my fortune. Now the pain melts away and, as the fog clears, that pale, pretty, delicate mask hangs before me again.

Lan Ping, Blue Apple. I make no excuses. I grew up where life hurt and my business was only to survive. It was my lover who tore the scales from my eyes and gave me to my greater purpose. He set me on my proper path when I signed the party oath at his side. I did not know then what part I would play; I was full of fire and fervour. When I gave my heart to the revolution, I left Lan Ping behind.

* * *

The Long March Home

It is evening now and the corridors are still. I can hear the hushed exchanges of the nurses. My throat is closing and my mouth is so dry that, if I could sleep again, I would. But a body dying by slow degrees is apt to lose its instinct for obedience so I stare instead into the shifting dark where his broad, flat face watches over me, floating disembodied in the air above my bed.

Its features are outlined in violet light, a ghastly, shimmering spectre. His eyes seem to challenge me, all accusation and reproach. I am too weak to shake my head but I wonder how he *dares* to reproach me. I only did what he did himself. Did he think that a woman could not be cruel, would falter and lack the strength? In the old days, he sometimes made that mistake, overlooking the trials of my girlhood. Though I lived for so long in the shadow of his greatness, I was not without ambition of my own.

After his lust for my body subsided, it is true that our quarrels grew spiteful. It is *also* true that we made a good team, both apart and side by side. He was a great man. I saw his greatness: that was the reason I chose him. Our love affair was no happy chance. It was all by my design.

First, I flattered him. I went to his lectures and sat in the very first row. I gazed at him with tender eyes; I nodded; I smiled. Then, at the end, I would clap and clap till my palms were red and tingling. When I knew his eyes were on me, I would turn my face away. In the next stage, I would visit his cave, carrying with me some paper or some question. After I had prepared his meal, I would sit like a dog at his feet. "I do not understand," I told him and he would stroke my hair and instruct me. I would not say I did not care for him at all but I felt most the passion of my power.

What does he *think,* I wonder, when he comes to me now and finds me so shrivelled and so wasted? Does he remember the curve of my thigh? Does he guess at the contents of my heart?

* * *

There are those who have said I was cruel and vindictive, that I looked for a personal revenge. But, if I

289

did – and I don't *say* that I did – who was it who taught me?

"The more people you kill," he said once, "the more revolutionary you are." Another time, "All bad persons are bad; if they are beaten to death, it doesn't matter." These are political lessons I learned at his knee. I persecuted my enemies, I made them suffer. I killed them when I had a mind to. But he, *he* killed thousands – he tortured them and killed them – while others found release in suicide. It's a viable solution. There is always the long march home.

Now the plotting and the killing and the key-note speeches have drifted into distant memory. *Always*, it was all about death and death will always be there. We distracted ourselves with our high-sounding phrases and the glory of our "Cultural Revolution". "To read too many books is harmful," our painted posters proclaimed.

But now it seems to me that we somehow missed the point. Our ancestors knew it: their literature, their "pernicious" art, gave death its proper place. Our glory,

290

as much as our cruelty, is a thin and pitiful clamouring. Always, it comes down in the end to the long and weary march home.

* * *

It is chilly here and the light is too bright. I can hear the nurses talking. Here is the rope that will take me back to the feet of my beloved Chairman Mao.

* * *

Al Claro de Luna

The girl took in a great gulp of air and offered up a silent prayer as she dropped to her knees on the icy flagstone floor. The stench of rotting flesh that filled her nostrils was almost more than she could stomach but she gritted her teeth, and breathing through her nose, did her utmost to conceal her disgust.

"Con su permiso, Señora," she said softly without lifting her eyes.

Her fingers worked deftly to expose the old woman's feet which had been heavily bandaged using strips of linen torn from discarded underskirts. Once white, these makeshift wrappings were now dirty, damp and fraying. It seemed likely that several days had passed since the wounds had been washed and dressed.

"Be careful, my child."

The warning came as she removed the last layer of linen. Much of the flesh that lay beneath it was swollen, red and raw. It oozed nastiness – thick yellow pus and a clear, watery fluid – while the smell was even more powerful, much worse than before. It was only on closer inspection, however, that the girl realised with horror that smallest toe on the left foot was altogether absent, leaving behind it a suppurating wound. Several of the remaining digits were more or less similarly corrupted. It was no wonder, she thought, that her patient was silent and tense with expectation: stiffly upright, dressed entirely in black, her face remained impassive; nevertheless, she could not help but flinch at even the gentlest of touches touch.

The girl felt her gorge rise but she struggled to control it, resolving to dedicate this act of service to the memory of her dead mother for the greater glory of whose sainted soul she would not turn away. It was only ten months since her mother's death as the result of a difficult confinement; her father, though, had wasted no time in taking a young and pretty bride. The motherless girl had failed to come to terms with this last and unlooked for misfortune. Grief-stricken, unwanted at home, and resentful of her step-mother's authority, she had first begged and then demanded to be allowed to enter Santa Clara's; more than that, she had refused all food until she had her way. When, at last, her father had consented, she had kissed his hand in gratitude. Shortly after, she took the name of Sor Chimène and gave herself up to God.

Now, though, she was down on her knees tending to the feet of a woman who had spent more than forty years locked up here in the castle of Tordesillas. Quite why this had happened the girl wasn't sure but the story went that, long ago, grief had driven her mad; indeed, just a few minutes earlier, Sor Angeles had implied that, quiet as she seemed, the woman was capable of "difficult" behaviour.

"She's not much of a conversationalist," the older nun had confided, "and, all things considered, I see no need to encourage it. The powers that be don't care for it at all so let's try to keep things as they are. Make her as comfortable as you can and try not to provoke her.

She's a temper on her when she wants to– though we
don't see so much of it now."

"Is she dangerous then?" Sor Chimène had
asked.

The older nun smiled.

"Sister, there is nothing to fear. I have been here
these seventeen years and, if ever she hurt anyone, it
was no one but her poor sad self."

"Es de dia o de noce?"

The words were hard to distinguish; the voice,
on the other hand, was not unpleasant but cracked from
lack of use.

"It is night time," said Sor Chimène, recovering
her composure, "there's a fine full moon above us."

"Ah, the moon, the beautiful moon – how long it
is since I have seen her. All these years, I have had no
window: they deny me even that."

Al Claro de Luna

"I could not bear to be without the moon," said the young nun impetuously. "When I look upon its lovely face, I am reminded of the beauty of Christ."

"You are young," said the woman, rasping, speaking slowly, "perhaps *too* young. You put me in mind of my Catalina before they took her away.

She paused then and looked all about her, as if imagining the open sky. Her expression was a mixture of remembered anguish and joy.

"I have not seen the moon these many years but it hangs like a jewel in my remembrance. I am reminded by it of nothing so much as the loss of my dear, dead husband and that last, long journey we made before he was laid to rest and lost to me forever."

Now Sor Chimène knew a little of this story but she was curious to find out more. At not quite fifteen years of age, she was still very young and these events touched on secret matters, things she was not supposed to know. She was aware that some people spoke solemnly of them while others laughed and leered: in their cups, the men joked together and the women looked severe.

And yet, thought Sor Chimène, here was a chance to find out the truth for, surely, there could scarcely be a more knowledgeable source than this. Her conscience niggled but she put to one side the fact that such gossip was forbidden. If she ignored the guilt and the need for confession and thought only in practical terms, then she had to admit that what Sor Angeles didn't know couldn't put her out of temper.

"What was he like, your husband," she said, "and how did he die?"

Here she stole a quick and furtive glance at her companion. The woman held herself so upright and still in her ancient black brocade that she resembled nothing quite so much as her own dark effigy.

"You must have loved him a great deal to remember him so – and to go on loving him still after all these years. I mean, you are very old, aren't you, even older, I think, than my great-grandmother?"

Blushing, she halted then and her voice trailed away. She was conscious that by speaking so freely she may have caused some offence. To cover her embarrassment she dipped a soft cloth into the water she had brought there for that purpose and began to dab lightly at the pale and puffy ankles, moving down the front of each foot and round towards its leathery sole. She took care to avoid the worst of the sores and the rotted and rotting toes. It was not by any means a pleasant task but she embraced it as a penance for her rudeness.

For some minutes, no more was said and the silence settled around them. This, she thought, is how this woman had passed almost the whole of her adult life. How could she bear it, to be locked up so long with so little light and no company? Was it true that, when they locked her up, she was less thirty years old?

As though in response to the girl's curiosity, the old woman stirred and spoke.

"I had ten years of marriage," she said, "and perhaps ten months of happiness. My beautiful husband was a good man but he played in the sunshine like a child. He was charming and full of sport but, sadly, he was also very weak. We were we happy at first, deliriously so, but always there was someone to tempt him. I spit on his mistresses, all of them – hussies and whores. What could they have known of passion's depths? What *did* they know of love?"

Sor Chimène was shocked to hear this outburst but she was also intrigued and excited. All these matters lay far beyond the bounds of her experience. For one thing, prior to her journey to the St Clara's, she had travelled scarcely at all and never more than a half a day's walking from her home on the outskirts of the village. Secondly, apart from her two second cousins who were peculiarly gawky and ill-favoured, she had had few opportunities to meet or mix with the young men of the village. It was true that, at Mass, they had winked and smiled, beckoned and blown her kisses; but then had come the day when her father had turned and caught her blushing and giggling. He had slapped her face so hard that night she had been quickly seen the folly of her ways.

"*I* know nothing of love, Seňora," the girl ventured to whisper.

It seemed to her there was a flicker of response from the remote and statue-like figure.

"It is a subject which, when I take my vows, must be closed to me forever, but I am ashamed to say there is something inside me that yearns to understand what I have lost."

There was a long silence in the space of which she bitterly regretted her words. What if this woman were to repeat them to Sor Angeles or, worse, to Mother Superior? Crazy she might very well be – and in the town they called her La Loca – but viciousness in the very old was not at all uncommon. Was it envy that prompted them to it and the shadow of their own mortality? Would she in her turn one day look on the young and feel nothing but spite and malice?

Once more, the deep, rasping voice broke through her thoughts. Sor Chimène was startled, even a little alarmed. Was it possible its owner could see into her heart and read there all her secret desires? She almost feared to raise her head lest she meet the woman's eye.

"I am an old, old woman with little time left on this earth but I do not fear death; on the contrary, I am impatient for it; I look for it every day. Through death's dark portal I must pass in faith to be reunited in grace with my husband – and I know he will love me in the afterlife as he did when first we met – as he *would* have done again had it not been for those who plotted and schemed against me."

"Father Miguel will not hear such things."

Sor Chimène was shocked.

"He would scold you and give you a penance – ten Hail Marys at least. We must make confession and afterwards put away such ideas. *In Heaven you will meet with your Saviour*, he says – here she spoke in a deep and solemn monotone – *so think not of your earthly loves. Those who turn their backs on Christ's perfect love will fall into eternal damnation.*"

La Loca shrugged her shoulders and for a moment her dark eyes flashed. "I have said my prayers," she said. "I have nothing to fear from my Saviour."

Then she leaned forward and lowered her voice.

"Listen – and learn from me – I will tell you everything. Hear my story and then decide what it is you have lost."

So Sor Chimène sat for as long as she dared at the feet of the Juana La Loca and heard at first-hand the story of her passion for Felipe el Hermoso. She heard how, long before the young nun's birth, the princess had taken ship for the Lowlands expecting a marriage of convenience and a life of duty and prayer. Instead, she found there a handsome young husband and passion that shaped her whole existence. Wrapped in his arms she came alive and, with his death, she died.

"But what of his mistresses," the younger woman asked, "how can you forgive him so many?"

"Do you not think it strange that you should ask me that, you above all other people? Does not your stern and earnest priest teach that forgiveness is all? It was *after* his death that I learned to forgive him, first as I kept vigil at Burgos. For five weeks I wept and prayed – I had some hope then of a miracle – eventually, though, when the fever came, I knew we had to go. Yes, I opened the casket. Why should I not? There were rumours that the body had been stolen. Afterwards, people some people made much of it –and my enemies used it against me – but, five weeks into my widowhood, it was natural enough, I think."

The young nun nodded a sympathy she was not quite convinced she should feel. *Was* it "natural" to open a coffin to adore a rotting corpse? But La Loca was warming to her subject now and her voice was growing steadily stronger. She leaned forward, drawing close to the girl and making a grab for her hand.

"We set out for Torquemada, then, en route to Grenada – and that was when I learned despair, compassion and forgiveness. I was heavily pregnant and we travelled by night to avoid the worst of the heat.

Al Claro de Luna

By the light of the moon, I talked to him; I showed him all the secrets of my heart."

"Your little girl, she was born to you then?"

The older woman paused. She inclined her head just a little to one side as though in the act of remembering.

"Yes, my Catalina," she said, "she was born in 1507. It was January. I sent them all away. She was my gift from God."

Sor Chimène flexed the fingers of her hand against the force of the older woman's grip. By the light of just the fire and two failing torches, it was impossible to be certain but she thought she saw a single tear roll down the bloated cheek. She felt a sudden impulse to kiss that cheek but there was no time left in which to do so. There was first the echo of quick sure steps, then the groan of the opening door.

"Come, Sister, it is growing late. You must surely be done by now."

Her mouth smiled but her tone was brisk and her eyes were hard and flat.

Sor Chimène nodded.

"Yes, Sister Angeles."

There was nothing else for it. With a last glance at Juana La Loca, she gathered up the water bowl and scurried out of the room.

But she loitered for a moment in the narrow passage, fearing what might happen next. She heard the heavy door creak shut and then the nun's raised voice.

"I will endure no more of your nonsense," she said, and, for it, you shall have no supper."

Sor Chimène retired to her cell where she stood at the open casement. For a very long while she looked up at the moon and wept over what she had lost.

* * *

Looking Back

acknowledgements

"Mama" by Tantra Bensko first appeared in *Between Altered States*, issue 7, November, 2010

"Bringing Back Beulah" by Carly Berg first appeared in *Devilfish Review*

"Fat Pat" by Carly Berg first appeared in *Free Flash Fiction*

"The Last Supper" by Carly Berg first appeared in *Orion Headless*

"Shattered" by Carly Berg first appeared in *Orion Headless*

"Risen" by Carly Berg first appeared in *Fiction 365*

"The Horse Head Earrings" by Carly Berg first appeared in *Untoward Magazine*

"Turquoise Dreams" by Carly Berg first appeared in *Here Comes Everyone*

"The Old Should Be Explorers" by Ute Carson first appeared in *PitWit.com*, 2006

"Just One More Thing (to go wrong)" by James D. Reed first appeared in *Midwestern Gothic,* issue #8

"The Storekeeper" by Tom Sheehan first appeared in his own collection of short fiction "Brief Cases, Short Spans", 2008

"Rig Runner" by Tom Sheehan first appeared in *Fiction Warehouse*, 2002

"The Long March Home" by Abigail Wyatt first appeared in her own collection of short fiction "Old Soldiers, Old Bones and Other Stories"

"Al Claro de Luna" by Abigail Wyatt first appeared in her own collection of short fiction "Old Soldiers, Old Bones and Other Stories"

Looking Back
table of contents

Nazar Look

Attitude and Culture Journal of Crimean Tatars in Romania
www.nazar-look.com

2013 Projects:

Looking Back
Anthology of Short Stories

Tomcat Tale by Valery Petrovsky
Short Story Collection (English / Romanian / Crimean Tatar editions)

Metric Conversions – Metrelí kaytarmalar
Poetry of Our Time - Búgúngí tízmeler ğîyîntîgî

2012 Projects:

The Bizarre Age
Anthology of Short Stories

Crossing the Path of Tellers
Short Stories of Our Time

The Infinite Facets of Sphere
An Anthology of Essays and Interviews

Magnetic Resonance Therapy
Anthology of Interviews

Spectral Lines
Anthology of Contemporary Poetry

Extraterrestrial Life
Poetry of Our Time